FIRST-JOB
Survival Guide
HOW TO THRIVE AND ADVANCE IN YOUR NEW CAREER

DIANE C. DECKER, VICTORIA A. HOEVEMEYER, *and* MARIANNE ROWE-DIMAS

JIST Works
America's Career Publisher

First-Job Survival Guide

© 2006 by Diane C. Decker, Victoria A. Hoevemeyer, and Marianne Rowe-Dimas

Published by JIST Works, an imprint of JIST Publishing, Inc.
8902 Otis Avenue
Indianapolis, IN 46216-1033
Phone: 1-800-648-JIST   Fax: 1-800-JIST-FAX   E-mail: info@jist.com

Visit our Web site at **www.jist.com** for information on JIST, free job search tips, book chapters, and ordering instructions for our many products! For free information on 14,000 job titles, visit **www.careeroink.com**.

> Quantity discounts are available for JIST books. Please call our Sales Department at 1-800-648-5478 for a free catalog and more information.

Acquisitions and Development Editor: Lori Cates Hand
Interior Designer: designLab
Page Layout: Carolyn J. Newland
Proofreaders: Linda Seifert, Jeanne Clark
Indexer: Kelly D. Henthorne

Printed in the United States of America
10 09 08 07 06 05   9 8 7 6 5 4 3 2 1

Library of Congress Cataloging-in-Publication Data
Decker, Diane C.
   First-job survival guide : how to thrive and advance in your new career /
   Diane C. Decker, Victoria A. Hoevemeyer, and Marianne Rowe-Dimas.
       p. cm.
   Includes index.
   ISBN 1-59357-253-0 (alk. paper)
   1. Youth—Employment—United States—Case studies. 2. Vocational
   guidance—United States—Case studies. I. Hoevemeyer, Victoria A. II.
   Rowe-Dimas, Marianne, 1949- III. Title.
   HD6273.D43 2006
   650.1—dc22
                                                        2005024684

ISBN 1-59357-253-0

About This Book

You're about to graduate and you're preparing to start your first "real" job. Or maybe you're already out there working and you're finding the adjustment to be a little more difficult than you expected. No fear—your survival guide is here!

First-Job Survival Guide is a unique, easy-to-read, reference guide that will give recent high school or college graduates who are new—or relatively new—to the workforce the practical, usable guidance and advice they need to thrive in the world of work. You'll learn from real stories, checklists, and self-tests based on the authors' extensive experience coaching people just like you to succeed on the job.

If you're starting your new job tomorrow, jump right into the Introduction, which gives helpful tips and pointers to make the day a great start to a long and satisfying career. Then you can read more about presenting a polished image at work (personally, in writing, and on the phone), business etiquette, dealing with difficult co-workers, developing a positive relationship with your boss, working well as part of a team, managing conflict, influencing others, and maximizing your results at work.

We wish you the best of luck in your new career!

Dedications

For my mother, Bettie Decker.

—Diane Decker

In memory of my brother, Jeff.

—Victoria Hoevemeyer

To my twin sister, Madonna, without whose inspiration, encouragement, and support my contribution to this book would not have been possible.

—Marianne Rowe-Dimas

Acknowledgments

From Diane:

I want to thank the following people for their generous contributions during the writing of this book. To Angie Massani and Kai Murray for offering experiences of new graduates in their first jobs. To Lori Cates Hand for her creative and positive approach to editing. To my co-authors, Marianne and Vicki, for collaboratively transforming breakfast conversations into this finished product. To my daughter, Kate, and son, Bret, for sharing their insights. To my husband, Jim, for patiently listening and helping me clarify my thoughts.

From Victoria:

Special thanks go to Mike Alagna for our many discussions, one of which led to the idea for this book.

From Marianne:

Thanks first to my husband, Ken, for always believing in me and supporting me in all my endeavors. Thanks also to Nicole Dimas for her comments and perceptions as a member of our target audience.

I am grateful to the human resource and training professionals who have shared with me the traits they consider desirable but often missing in newly hired graduates. I also appreciate the observations given me by the people in my communications classes and business training sessions. Your insights have been most valuable.

Finally, I am forever indebted to my sister, Madonna, for her invaluable input and editorial expertise. I also appreciate the great deal of time she spent reading and editing and reading again.

CONTENTS

INTRODUCTION

Surviving Your Very First Day on the Job

T he alarm goes off. You look over and see it's 5:45 a.m. You want to roll over and go back to sleep but...it's your first day on the job!

After all the years you have spent in school, the world of work is looming in front of you. Now reality hits—it's off to a world so different than school that it's like entering another galaxy. Project timeframes are going to shrink from lasting a month to just a week or a day. There will be no more sleeping late in the morning. Well-worn jeans, a t-shirt, and athletic shoes will give way to—at minimum—business-casual dress. Experimenting with different shades of purple, green, or red hair dye will be better left as a fond memory of your youth.

Feeling a little nervous? Wondering if you're going to be able to do what you've been hired to do? You're not alone. Just the thought of starting a new job can make even experienced employees a little nervous!

This chapter will provide you with guidance to make your first few weeks—especially that critical first day—less nerve-wracking. And this book, as a whole, will fill you in on what it takes to be successful. But let's start at the beginning. The first impression you make when you walk into your new place of employment can be a lasting one. That means you need to think about—and plan for—your first day of work ahead of time.

Before Your First Day

In order to be prepared to start your new job, there are at least four things that you need to do: research your new employer, time and plan your route to work, check your wardrobe, and adapt your sleep habits. Let's explore each of these.

1. Research Your New Employer

Although you might have done research on your new employer as part of the job search and interview process, it might not have been in-depth. Now that you are going to work for the company, you need to take time to learn about your new employer. Find out what the product or service lines are; how your employer is different than its competitors; what the organization's vision, mission, values, and ethics statements are; what the history of the company is; what the company's financial statements look like, and similar information. If you received an annual report or any other company literature during the interview process, read it. If not, search the company's Web site for the answers to these questions. Don't forget to check with your friends, family, and other associates to see whether they are familiar with the company or know anyone who works there.

You may also want to gather some less formal, but just as important data. For example, when do people typically start the day and when do they leave? On your first day, you most likely will leave at a decent hour, but you should be willing to stay longer if needed. Also, find out what people do for lunch and bring enough money based on what you learn.

2. Time and Plan Your Route to Work

Take time to commute to your new workplace during rush hour at least once before you start the job. This trial run will give you a more realistic estimate of the time you need to leave for work on your first day. You might also want to check out a couple different routes that you could take, in case of an accident, bad weather, traffic lights being out, or other calamities.

3. Check Your Wardrobe

Think about what clothes you want or need to wear to work (see the "Dress Appropriately" section later in this chapter). You might find that appropriate work attire is significantly different from what you wore in school. As a result, you might have to go shopping for a few things to get you started.

If you have clothes that are appropriate for work, take them out of your closet and make sure they are clean, pressed, and in good repair. If they need cleaning, wash them or take them to the dry cleaner. Repair clothing with loose or missing buttons, open seams, or rips. Don't wait until the last minute to take care of these things.

Carin Should Have Checked Her Clothes

Carin knew what she wanted to wear to work the first day, and took it out of her closet after her morning shower. She was still tired from not getting a good night's sleep, so she didn't really pay attention as she was getting dressed. Her new boss met her as she entered the building. As she started to shake her boss's hand, she noticed a large stain on the cuff of her jacket that anyone shaking her hand would see. There was no way of hiding it, so every time she shook hands with someone her first day, the stain glaringly stood out. Had she checked the suit jacket the week before, she could have cleaned it and avoided the embarrassment.

---

4. Adapt Your Sleep Habits

One of the most challenging aspects of the transition from school to work can be the hours of work, if you need to wake up earlier than usual. You might have arranged your class schedule to avoid 8:00 a.m. classes, but now you won't have that option. It might take some time for your body clock to readjust, so begin waking up and going to bed earlier at least a week before your first day. This adjustment process will help you to stay alert during the entire day.

Sara Dozes Off in a Meeting

Unfortunately, Sara did not plan ahead before she started her job at a manufacturing facility one month after her graduation. During that month, she maintained the late schedule that she became accustomed

(continued)

(continued)

to during her last semester of classes. She was expected to be at work by 7:30 a.m. Sara didn't mind the early start time, even though she normally didn't go to sleep until after midnight. But Sara's difficulty occurred about 1:30 each afternoon. While in training meetings with her new boss, she found it impossible to stay focused and alert. In fact, during a review of budget figures, Sara actually drifted off. This meeting was one of those embarrassing moments that is tough to laugh about, even years later. For some people, it could be even more than an embarrassing moment—it could well lead to the end of the new job.

On Your First Day

It's not as easy as just rolling out of bed, into the shower, into your clothes, and out the door. On your first day, keep in mind the following: allow extra time to get to work, dress appropriately, remember names, make the most of your orientation, and smile and be friendly.

1. Allow Extra Time to Get to Work

Even if you made a test run during rush hour, allow extra time to get to work. It's important that you allow for emergencies—such as accidents—that might delay you, as well as allowing time for the important things, like running into Starbucks. If you get to the office too early, you can always wait in your car, which is preferable to the negative image you will create by arriving late.

2. Dress Appropriately

If you haven't been told what the company's dress code is, contact your boss or human resources prior to your start day and ask what the dress guidelines are. What you wear, especially on your first day of work, is important because people will be making decisions about you based on your physical appearance—and your clothing is a big part of your physical appearance. You need to find a balance between being overdressed and appearing too casual. In general, dress at the top level of—or slightly above—what is expected of employees at your level. Wearing the right clothing will also help ease your nervousness.

3. Remember Names

You are going to meet many new people—managers, co-workers, and perhaps even clients. With so many new names being thrown at you, you might be concerned that you'll forget most of them. There is a lot of value in taking the extra effort to remember names. People admire and respect those who remember their names, and you will make a great impression if you are able to do so.

If you have trouble remembering names, try these techniques:

- Remember a person's name through the use of your senses: hearing, seeing, and speaking. When you are introduced to Manuel Martinez, for example, you *hear* his name. Then, you can *speak* his name by saying, "It's nice to meet you, Manuel." If you have a few minutes to talk to him, you might end your conversation with, "I look forward to working with you Manuel." Also, if it's appropriate, ask for his business card. Look at the name on the card before you put it in your pocket or card case. *Seeing* the name in print is a visual reminder in addition to hearing and saying the name. The more senses you use, the more likely you are to remember a person's name.

- Associate a person's name with something or someone you know or link it with something that will jog your memory the next time you see the person. It takes some time to develop this skill, but it is especially helpful in name recall. The following Name Association chart gives some examples of how this technique might work.

Name Association

Person's Name	Association
Norma	Norma is a very normal looking and acting person, so you think, to yourself, "Normal Norma." or "Norma is normal." or "Norma looks normal, acts normal, and talks normal."
Mandy Harrison	You notice that she wears a lot of makeup, so you might remember her by using her initials—MH—to come up with a phrase (for example, "Make-up: heavy") that will help you remember her name.

The association you use doesn't have to make sense to anyone other than yourself. Although there is no hard-and-fast rule that the association has to be flattering to the person, you should exercise caution in using negative associations because, for most of us, our thoughts have a strong impact on our interactions with and perceptions of others.

Be ready to introduce yourself to colleagues if your boss does not take the time to do so. Take the initiative to go up to others to show your friendliness and excitement about working there. Your positive energy can be contagious to others you will be interacting with in the future.

4. Make the Most of Your Orientation

Try to learn as much as you can about who and what will be covered during your orientation. This pre-work will help you figure out the questions that you want answered so that you can bring them with you the first day. If the leaders of your orientation provide guidelines for how and when they want questions asked, make sure you abide by them as you ask your questions.

Be careful not to monopolize the question-and-answer part of the orientation. You want to strike a balance between showing sincere interest in what is being shared and being annoyingly self-centered on your own issues. If there are questions of a personal nature, you might want to ask these of the appropriate person outside of the orientation meeting.

Be prepared for a meeting with a human resource representative to complete paperwork. You will most likely be given tax and insurance forms to complete. Be sure to bring your Social Security number and a photo ID with you so that you can confirm your eligibility to work in the U.S. and so that your tax documents can be set up correctly. If you are overwhelmed or confused by any documents you are given, request some time to review them at home. Ask for any supplemental materials that will help explain what is required. Take the papers home and discuss your questions with others you trust, making sure to return them to human resources by the date required.

5. Smile and Be Friendly

People are much more likely to approach a smiling person than one who frowns. Also think about being the person who brings a smile to other people's faces. That doesn't mean being the corporate version of a class clown; simply be cheerful. If you're not introduced by your boss or one of your co-workers to those who work around you, put on a smile and introduce yourself to them.

After Your First Day

Although surviving the first day on a new job is an achievement, it's only the start of your career and the beginning of what you need to learn about your job, your co-workers, your department, and your company. To be successful, consider doing the following during the first few weeks—and even months—of your career.

1. Ask Questions

No one will expect you to have all the answers—not for the first few days and perhaps not for the first few weeks! The only way you are going to find out about the company, how everything works, and what you are supposed to do is by asking questions. Others are not going to think that you are stupid if you ask questions. Quite the opposite tends to be true.

Leroy Should Have Asked More Questions

During his last year in school, Leroy had worked nights in the copy center of the company he was eventually hired into as a full-time, entry-level analyst. He figured that he learned what he needed to know about the company during his part-time stint. Leroy assumed that the expectations of his boss and others would be that he wouldn't have many questions.

Unfortunately, Leroy found that his part-time night job and his daytime analyst position were quite different, and he had a lot of questions. Because he was afraid that people would think that he should already know the answers, he didn't ask questions. Some people saw his silence as him being a know-it-all, while others simply saw him as being stuck-up. It took Leroy about a month to realize that his failure to ask questions was having a negative impact on his ability to develop good working relationships and could, if it continued, potentially hurt his career. Once he started asking questions and checking his assumptions, his entire work experience began to improve.

---

2. Keep a Journal

Think about keeping a log or journal, starting your first day and continuing through your first few weeks on the new job. Record your first impressions, questions, concerns, and delights, as well as information you gather about who does what in the company, the organization's culture, and other information you receive on how to be successful in the company. You will be bombarded with so much information that it can be difficult to immediately process it all. Taking time to jot down notes during the day or at the end of the day will ensure that you recall important insights that will be helpful to look back on in the future. In addition, the process of writing can help to clarify your thoughts and provide insights on the actions you may want to take.

It is wise to keep this journal private. Although public journals as part of online blogs are very popular, your company will most likely not appreciate its employees sharing personal insights about the company culture, nor sharing company secrets, with the vast world of Internet users. Many well-known companies have fired workers because of the content of their blogs.

3. Learn from Your Mistakes

Recognize that everyone makes mistakes. The mark of a true professional, though, is to catch the mistake, admit to it, take corrective action, learn from the mistake, and not repeat it. If you're lucky, you may be able to work for someone whose philosophy is "If you're not making three mistakes a year, you're not doing your job." If you're repeating the same mistake, though, you may soon not have a job to do!

Beyond Your First Day

There are myriad other factors to consider, many of which we've addressed in later chapters of this book. The content of this book is based on the feedback we have received from executives, human resource professionals, hiring managers, recently hired individuals, and our own personal experiences. Each chapter addresses a different set of skills that are highly desired in new hires.

You've made the right first step in surviving and thriving in your new job by choosing to read this book. Learn and apply the lessons it contains. These lessons are designed to help you be more capable and successful in your job. The chapters provide knowledge to help you develop skills in areas that are essential for new hires to develop. Although they won't—by themselves—guarantee you a perfect start to your career, they are the bedrock essentials that will put you a step ahead of other new employees.

Congratulations on your new job. We wish you the best of luck in starting your career. And, don't forget—if you haven't already done so—make sure to take time to celebrate this significant milestone in your life!

PART 1

It's All About Image

CHAPTER 1 Your Professional Image

You must have made a great first impression during your interview, or you wouldn't have gotten the job. Keep up the good work because there are more people you will need to impress, beginning with the people you didn't meet during your interview. They are your co-workers and company managers. In rare instances, this group may even include your boss. Your first day of work is even more important if you haven't previously met your boss, as this is when his or her first impression of you will be made. If your job entails client contact, as most customer service and sales jobs do, you'll have to consider how to impress your clients, as well.

Experts continue to stress how important first impressions are and how quickly they are made. In general, from between seven seconds to four minutes of having met you, assumptions are made (whether correct or incorrect) about your economic status, self-assurance, credibility, educational level, and more. The first impression others have of you is especially important because although it takes very little time to make, a first impression is lasting. It is unlikely that you will get a chance to undo the damage of a botched first impression, so be sure that you do it right the first time.

Making Good First Impressions

We all want to make a good impression on others, but in order to do so, it's necessary to consider the factors that are involved. There are three major considerations. They have to do with how you look, how you sound, and what you say.

- How you look—the visual impression you give—is based on your overall appearance and your body language.

- How you sound—the way that you speak—includes your rate of speech, volume, pitch, and vocal variation.

- What you say—your spoken language—concerns the words that you actually speak.

All three of these factors contribute to the overall impression you give others, and they can either enhance or detract from your professional image.

In his book *Silent Messages,* Professor Albert Mehrabian found that when an inconsistent message is given, the visual expression has a greater impact on the total message than the vocal or verbal expression. He states that "appearance and especially nonverbal mannerisms can significantly contribute to the impression one makes." For instance, let's say that your boss gives you a new project that she expects completed in a short period of time. You are already overwhelmed by your current workload. You may respond with, "Thanks, I'm really excited to be given this project and will make sure that it is completed on schedule." Those are the words that you speak, but if your facial expression is one of panic and the tone of your voice doesn't sound truly excited, your words won't be believed.

If your co-workers are favorably impressed the first time they meet you, that impression will have a positive affect on how they view you in the future. In order to keep that positive impression going, however, you need to be consistent. "Consistent in what way?", you may ask. First, you need to be consistent on a daily basis. For instance, with regard to your visual appearance, if you look crisp, clean, and put-together two days of the week, and rumpled, frumpy, and disheveled the other three, you are sending a mixed message about yourself. Mixed messages are open to interpretation; they can open the door to an erosion of the good first impression you worked so hard to create. Second, you should be consistent with how you want others to perceive you. For example, if you are at a mid-management level but dress more like an entry-level employee, your visual appearance is not consistent with your position.

The rest of this chapter goes into detail about how to make good visual, vocal, and verbal impressions.

How You Look

The moment you step through the door and enter a room, you are sending a strong message to those present—a message about how professional you are. From your bearing, to your grooming, to your dress, people judge you based on your outward appearance. They say, "You can't judge a book by its cover," but we all do. The more attractive the dust jacket, the more likely the book is to sell. Ours is a fast-paced world, one in which people often make rapid-fire decisions about other people based on initial perceptions. In order for you to be successful, you must be aware of what contributes to the perceptions others have of you.

Your clothing, grooming, and body language can either contribute to or detract from your professional presence. The following guidelines and·tips will help you to present an effective business image.

Business-Casual Attire

It's not as easy as it once was to get dressed for work. In the past, things were a lot simpler—more uncomfortable, but a lot simpler. Professional men, for instance, went to their closets and chose from a selection of basic business suits in basic colors. They then chose a white or pale-colored shirt and a subtle tie. Most selections could be easily matched and choices were extremely limited. This allowed for a fast sweep of the closet, and few real decisions. In retrospect, at 6:30 in the morning, fast and easy had definite advantages.

Ladies had more choices with regard to their clothing and could add interest with jewelry, a colorful blouse, or a scarf, but even their choices were certainly not as extensive as they currently are.

Most companies today do not require formal business attire. Men and women in a wide variety of fields and positions are able to wear business-casual attire. It's certainly more comfortable (the reason most people tend to prefer it), but it can have drawbacks. Business-casual attire means more choices, not just in the types of clothes you may choose, but also regarding fabric, color, pattern, and texture. People now have to figure out what goes with what.

Business-Casual for Men

For men, the key is to choose business basics, but these basics now include pants in twill, wool, microfiber, linen, or fabric blends.

Shirts can be peach, bright yellow, French blue, gingham check, or other bright choices, and you can choose to top your shirt with a sport coat, blazer, vest, or sweater.

Wow! Options! Choices! Decisions! You want a look that's modern and fashionable, but one that means business, and you definitely don't have it as easy as your dad's generation when it comes to getting dressed and looking professional.

Business-Casual for Women

Women have their own challenges. There are myriad clothing choices, many of which are appealing but not appropriate for work. A blouse made of a clingy material, especially if it is low cut, may be appropriate to wear after work with friends; but if it is worn during work or in the company of co-workers after work, it sends the wrong message. Ask any working woman whether she would like to be viewed as a sex object by managers, co-workers, and clients. Most, if not all, would reply, "Of course not. I want to be considered as a competent professional." If that is truly what you want, you will have to dress the part. It is difficult to be taken seriously when you are wearing a low-cut, clingy blouse with a miniskirt and stiletto heels. Low-rise pants, especially when combined with cropped tops, also send the wrong message. Pants that fall a little below the waist are fine if they are paired with a tucked-in blouse or a longer tunic top, so that when you bend over, your skin (or thong!) doesn't show.

Business-casual dress for today's woman may include dresses, pantsuits, jumpers, slacks, skirts, vests, blazers, blouses, knit tops, and sweaters. The options and combinations of these items are considerable, especially when purchased as separates with mixing and matching in mind.

Help Is Available!

If you just don't know where to begin in assembling a business-casual wardrobe that works for you, there is help. The staff in most quality department stores is knowledgeable and helpful. Many of these stores also have personal shoppers to help their customers, and this service is free. You may also want to obtain the services of an image consultant. To find information on how to obtain the services of an image consultant, visit www.aici.org, the official Web site for the Association of Image Consultants International.

Consider the Company Culture

Both men and women should consider the culture of the company when choosing what to wear. If it is a law office or financial institution, you may be wearing a formal business suit or find that a jacket is required. In fields such as marketing, publishing, retail, transportation, food service, travel, and so on, khakis teamed with a collared shirt may be considered appropriate business attire for most people in the organization. In communications, technology, education, and health care, dress codes may be even more relaxed, with jeans and athletic shoes allowed.

There is much variation, and a dress code is ultimately decided upon by each individual company. Of course, in any organization, your position and whether or not you have client contact influences what you wear. In banking, a bank manager may regularly wear a suit, while tellers will most likely be dressed more informally—men in pants and a shirt, ladies in a skirt or slacks paired with a sweater set or blouse.

How do you know that you are dressing properly? Do your research and be observant. Most companies and organizations provide dress guidelines in their employee manuals. If you are not given this information with your orientation materials, ask human resources for guidance. Dress guidelines, when given, are expected to be followed, so read them carefully. Look at how others are dressed, especially managers and those who are respected by management. Follow their lead. Although some company dress codes cover six or more pages, most are short and give just a brief overview. You are expected to take these guidelines, generalize them, and make intelligent decisions regarding clothing choices. Remember that the dress codes established by a company normally represent the minimum standard expected. When in doubt about a clothing choice, it is probably the wrong choice. Don't wear it!

Dress Appropriately for Planned Activities

Another thing to consider when dressing for work is what's on your calendar for the day. Would you wear a three-piece business suit and dress shoes if you were taking a customer to a baseball game? Not if you could avoid it. Neither would this type of attire be appropriate for a company picnic or golf outing. On the other hand, if you are giving a presentation to upper management or visiting your client's office, you would most likely opt for more formal business attire. The type of clothing you wear should be determined by what activities are planned for the day, taking into consideration dress code guidelines.

Make Sure It Fits

Good-fitting clothes are essential to a good business image. You don't want to look as if you're wearing your older brother's or sister's hand-me-downs. In addition to looking more professional, you will look more trim and fit in well-tailored clothing. In general, more men than women have their clothes tailored, so women especially need to pay more attention to this aspect of their visual impression. It is the final touch that makes a big difference in how you are perceived.

The Impact of Color

Color also plays a part in business-casual dress. Wearing the right colors—those that complement your complexion—helps you look more alert and more refreshed. If you don't know what colors look best on you, ask a friend for advice or have an expert give you a color consultation.

Build your business-casual wardrobe on a solid base of neutral business colors. Make your choices based on the colors that complement you, choosing from black, gray, brown, navy, camel, beige, olive, tan, and taupe. You can accent these basic neutrals with color. Note that subtle, subdued, toned-down accent colors make you appear more professionally dressed. Bright, clear colors, especially if they appear in patterns or flashy prints, give a more casual look.

Grooming

Your clothing may be of the highest quality and may fit properly, but if your grooming is not up to par, the entire picture you're presenting is negatively affected. Good grooming encompasses everything from your hair and makeup to your clothing, shoes, and, yes, even your underwear. Let's begin with grooming guidelines to help you look your best from top to bottom and inside out.

Hair

Hair for both men and women should be clean and fresh looking, not oily, matted, or disheveled. Hair should have a good cut and an up-to-date style. The bed head is definitely out! If you arrive for work with hair that looks as if you just rolled out of bed, the impression you give is that you can't organize your time well. It also indicates that you have very little regard for yourself, your company, and the people you work with. If you have difficult hair to work with or don't like working with it, get a hairstyle that is simple and easy to care for. If you color your hair, do it in natural colors (no green, pink, or purple) and touch it up regularly. Having an inch of outgrowth is not attractive and it detracts from your overall image.

Regarding facial hair, men should shave regularly. If your beard is particularly heavy, you may need to bring an electric shaver to work for a quick touch up, especially if you have an after-hours business function. Men who have beards, moustaches, or both should be sure that they are always neatly trimmed and combed.

Makeup

Less is more. Some people come to work looking like they're going out for a gala evening event, or worse, like they are going to a Halloween party. When putting on your makeup, use a light hand. Remember, it's daytime and you are going to work. On the other hand, some women wear no makeup at all. A little makeup helps you look more businesslike. Even if you don't regularly wear makeup, make a habit of wearing it to work. A light dusting of blush, colored lip gloss, and mascara will define your features and give you a more professional appearance.

Tattoos and Piercings

Your company may provide information on its policy regarding tattoos and piercings in the employee manual or in the dress code guidelines. If so, be sure to follow what is outlined. If your company doesn't give specifics, be aware that piercings (depending on what type and where they're located) and tattoos are not professional looking. If you have tattoos, they should be covered while you're at work. Piercings, other than a reasonable number in the ears, are generally frowned upon. Observe others in responsible positions and follow their lead regarding tattoos and piercings.

Hands

Whether you know it or not, your hands attract a great deal of attention, particularly while you're seated at a conference table during meetings. Both men and women should attend to their nails, making sure that nails and cuticles are trimmed, and that there is no dirt beneath nails or around cuticles. Nails with chipped or worn polish are unattractive and unprofessional looking. The darker the polish, the more obvious it is when it is chipped. If you have a busy lifestyle and don't have time for daily touchups, wear polish in a soft, neutral tone so that chips aren't as obvious. If you break a nail, trim the others so that the difference is not so apparent. Nails of vastly varying lengths do not look well groomed. Very long, dragon-lady nails are unprofessional looking, as are black or neon-colored nails, and those covered in glitter, jewels, and designs.

Clothing

Your clothes should be clean, pressed, and odor free. Check for stains before putting your clothes away, and check again before you put them on. Some stains aren't visible until they remain on clothing for a period of time.

Also, there is no excuse for wrinkled clothing. With the new wrinkle-free fabrics, spray-on wrinkle removers, tumble-press settings on clothes dryers, and ready availability of dry-cleaning, it's easier than ever to avoid a rumpled look. Seatbelts can be a problem, especially for jackets, so hang your jacket on the hook above the back door of your car or carefully fold and lay your jacket across the back seat. When you arrive at your destination, your jacket will look as freshly pressed as when it left your closet.

Washing or dry-cleaning your clothes frequently helps avoid clothing odors. Wear a shirt, blouse, or knit top only once between washings. Jackets, skirts, and pants should be laundered or dry-cleaned as needed to remove not just dirt and stains, but body oils and odors as well.

Hosiery

Some companies do not insist that their women employees wear nylons to work, especially during the summer months. Because you always look more professional if you wear hosiery, consider wearing nylons, even if it is not required by your dress code. Offices are air-conditioned and summer-weight pantyhose are available, so even on the hottest days, hosiery is not that uncomfortable to wear. Be sure that if you are wearing open-toed shoes, your hosiery has a sheer toe rather than a reinforced toe.

Men's socks and women's pantyhose should be in a shade that coordinates with the hemline of the skirt or pants being worn, as well as the shoes. Ladies should be alert for runs in their nylons as well as snags, which are especially noticeable when you're wearing darker hosiery. Always have a back-up pair of pantyhose in your desk drawer or purse for use in emergencies. If you wear patterned nylons, the pattern should be very subtle.

Underwear

We wear underwear for a variety of reasons: to support, to conceal, and to help our outer clothing lay better and look better. The first thing to remember is that although your underwear serves an important purpose, it is not meant to be seen.

No one should be able to see even the outline of your underwear. Colored or patterned panties that show through light or white pants are unacceptable, as are slips peeking out at the bottom of hemlines. No one should be able to tell what color your bra is or whether you're wearing a thong. To be sure that your underwear becomes nobody's business but yours, check yourself in front of a full-length mirror at home. Stoop, bend, and stretch in a variety of positions to be sure that your underwear is not visible at work, even if you're searching for a folder in the bottom file drawer.

Shoes

Do wear closed-toed shoes. They are more professional than open-toed shoes and sandals. Ladies may wear sandals in warm weather (dress code permitting). Choose ones that look businesslike, and make sure that you have regular pedicures. Men should wear sandals in only the most informal of business settings, and only if the dress code permits. Shoes you wear to work should be in neutral tones such as black, brown, cordovan, tan, and beige, and they should coordinate with your clothing. Women can add other subtle colors that match what they're wearing. If your company allows athletic shoes, they should be clean and in good condition.

Don't wear beach sandals or "flip-flops," shoes or boots with stiletto heels, dirty or scuffed shoes, shoes with salt stains, or shoes with rundown heels.

Body Odors

Be watchful for body odors that can be offensive to those around you. Since the typical office has a large number of cubicles occupying a small amount of space, people work very closely together, and even mild body odors can be detected. If you smoke, be aware that tobacco odor is offensive to many and that it lingers not just on your breath, but also on your hands and clothing. Smoking isn't the only thing that contributes to bad breath—garlicky and spicy foods do, too. If you must indulge in very spicy foods, be sure to brush your teeth, gargle, and use a good breath deodorizer after eating.

If you like to workout over the lunch hour, allow enough time for a shower before returning to work. You might not be aware of your perspiration odor, but others will notice. Also, perspiration odors cling to clothing, so make sure that you have a fresh change of clothes and underwear to put on after your workout.

A little perfume or after-shave goes a long way. Be aware that your fragrance lingers long after you can no longer detect it. People often freshen their scent when there is no need to do so. Be aware of the fact that many people are sensitive to fragrance, others are allergic to it, and still others just don't like it or may not like the particular scent you're wearing.

Body Language

The silent language spoken by your body speaks volumes about you, and the more you know about this language and how to "speak" it, the more successful you will be. As mentioned earlier, many communication experts consider body language more important than the spoken word. Since most people lie better with words than with their bodies, astute observers can tell a lot about what a person is really thinking by observing silent body clues. Manage the impression others have of you by managing the messages your body sends.

Lack of Eye Contact Equals Loss of Job

Tori decided to apply for an open position in another department at her company. The position seemed ideally suited to her, and she wanted it very badly. During her interview with the department manager, Tori was very nervous. She felt too intimidated to look the manager directly in the eye, so for much of the interview, she looked at either the conference table or the floor. Because she didn't give her interviewer good eye contact, he viewed Tori as lacking confidence and having poor self esteem. Tori was not offered the job.

There are four key elements that comprise your body language: eye contact, posture, gestures, and facial expressions.

Eye Contact

People like and trust people who look them in the eye. How long should you maintain eye contact with someone? Normally, you should give sustained eye contact of about four to eight seconds. It will become apparent when you or the other person starts to feel uncomfortable. At that time, you need to glance away briefly. Also, you don't have to look directly at another person's eyes the entire time you are conversing. In fact, it's fine to move around the central area of the face, which includes the eyes and nose. Occasionally, you may want to expand your gaze to include the person's forehead, mouth, and chin. If your gaze remains in the triangular area between a person's eyes and nose, that person will most likely not be able to tell whether you are looking directly into his eyes.

If you feel uncomfortable looking directly into someone's eyes, look instead at the bridge of the nose. What you don't want to do is to look over a person's shoulder, at the ceiling, or at the floor. It is fine to look away for very short periods, but remember to return to the person's face.

If the person you're speaking to seems uncomfortable with a normal amount of eye contact, it may be due to a cultural difference. Many Asians prefer shorter eye contact, whereas Arabs and Latin Americans often prefer longer eye contact. Be sensitive to the person you are speaking with and gauge the amount of eye contact that is comfortable for him or her.

Exercise: Eye Contact

Talk to a friend or family member about something of interest to you for approximately two minutes. Ask your conversational partner to give you good, natural eye contact for the first 45 seconds to one minute that you are speaking. Then, for the remainder of the time you are talking, ask him or her to give sporadic eye contact. He or she may look over your shoulder, out the window, at the ceiling, or toward the floor for portions of the last minute you are speaking, alternating with giving you good eye contact. After you are finished talking, discuss how you felt the first minute compared to the final minute. Most people feel ignored or as if they are boring the other person when eye contact is withdrawn completely or given only sporadically.

People like you to pay attention to them. They like to feel that what they are saying is important and that they are important. Giving good eye contact is critical to good communication because it tells others that we are interested in them and in their message.

Posture

Your posture can be observed from quite a distance—from across a room, even from across a street. It's one of the first things that people notice about you, and they will make judgments about you based upon it. If you walk into a client meeting with your shoulders rounded and head bent slightly forward, you are communicating a lack of confidence and poor self-esteem. That is definitely not the message you want to send—EVER! Standing up straight (but not poker stiff) with your shoulders back and your head up lets people know that you are a confident individual, alert and self assured, who respects herself as well as others.

One of the things people often forget about good posture is that it should be practiced while seated as well as while standing. In an office situation, you will often be seated, and unfortunately, slouching or slumping is the typical posture that employees exhibit while seated at their desks or while they are in meetings. Whenever you are seated, remember to sit up straight, and don't lounge with your feet up on the desk or another chair. If you want to make a great impression, don't slouch! Wait to relax until you get home and stretch out on the couch.

In addition to your posture, the way you walk can contribute to or detract from your overall professional presence. A very slow walk, or one in which you are dragging your feet, sends the message to others that you are lazy, tired, depressed, unmotivated, or at the very least, not happy to be where you are. If your walk is too fast, you look harried, stressed out, or unable to manage your time. Neither of these two types of walk will advance your career. Instead, walk briskly and purposefully with good posture. This is a winning combination that says you are efficient, energetic, positive, and upbeat.

Exercise: Posture

Place a full-length mirror in a room, against a far wall. Enter the room opposite the mirror and walk toward it as if you were at work. Observe your posture. Are your shoulders back, your head held up and your back straight? What about your stride? Is it at an energetic but unhurried pace? Do you look like you are a go-getter who means business? If not, practice until that is the impression you give as you walk toward the mirror.

Gestures

We generally gesture using our hands, arms, heads, or all three in combination. Gestures add life to what we are saying and can help us emphasize points we want to make. Some people gesture quite a bit, others very little. Using gestures effectively is not so much about how you gesture as it is about how natural your gestures are and whether they support what you're saying.

There are two gestures to avoid. The first is finger pointing. It is rude and it makes the person on the receiving end feel as if he or she is being scolded. The other gesture, folding your arms across your chest, makes you look defensive or as if you want to distance yourself. Uncross your arms and lower them to your sides for an open body stance that makes you appear friendly and approachable.

Facial Expressions

Our faces are open books, ready to be read by one and all. Facial expressions help others better understand our verbal message. They help impart the true meaning of what we want to say and they assist us in sharing our feelings and emotions.

There are two main things to remember about facial expressions:

- **Your facial expressions must coordinate with what you are saying or what another person is saying to you.** If you are expressing confusion or doubt about something you've heard, your eyebrows would most likely be knitted together, and your mouth drawn in a straight line or pursed. You certainly wouldn't have an inappropriate expression such as both eyebrows raised high and your mouth wide open. The latter expression would be appropriate if you had heard something totally surprising or shocking. Some people are not aware that their facial expressions don't match what they're saying or what they're hearing.

- **Your facial expressions should never indicate that you are being sarcastic, condescending, or disdainful.** That little smirk or roll of the eyes may not be observed by the person being derided, but be assured that others will observe and judge you negatively.

Exercise: Facial Expressions

Sit or stand in front of a mirror while you are speaking on the phone. Observe your facial expressions. Are your expressions appropriate reflections of what you are saying and what you are hearing from the other person? Do you observe any annoying or distracting things about your expressions that you'd like to change?

How You Sound

Your vocal impression is formed by how you speak, not what you say. How your voice sounds strongly impacts how others perceive you. There are many factors that contribute to your vocal image. Pitch, intonation, rate, and volume are four that you should consider.

Pitch

This refers to how high or low the tone of your voice is. Be aware that a very high-pitched voice is not as pleasant to listen to as a lower-pitched voice. In addition, if your pitch is too high, you will probably be viewed as being nervous, even if you are not. This is because when people are nervous, their voice pitch tends to go up. Finally, men and women with very high-pitched voices may be viewed as being less credible than those with a lower pitch.

Intonation

Having an even pitch, evenly timed words, lack of emphasis, and insufficient pauses leads to speaking in a monotone. Think of the classroom teachers you had who spoke in a monotone. BORING! They probably put you to sleep, as you will others if you don't strive to speak with some energy and variety in your voice. This can be achieved by varying the level of your voice from a higher to a lower pitch, pausing occasionally, and emphasizing certain words for effect.

Exercise 1: Intonation

Tape-record yourself for approximately five minutes. Don't read out of a book, just talk about a subject or tell a story that you know well. Replay the tape, listen to yourself, and ask a friend to honestly evaluate you. If you determine that you tend to speak in a monotone, work on adding variation to your speech. A good place to start is by listening to people you know, at work or in social situations, who you think speak well. Also, pay close attention to newscasters on television and on the radio. What about their delivery makes them easy to listen to, and what helps keep you interested in what they have to say? By carefully observing these experts, you can learn much about how to make your voice sound more varied and more interesting.

Exercise 2: Intonation

Find a story in the newspaper and read it through silently. Next, read through it again silently, but in your mind think how you might read it aloud if you were a newscaster. Finally, tape yourself reading the story aloud. When you replay the tape, critique yourself and find areas in which you need to improve. Work on one area at a time, allowing as much time as you need. For instance, you may want to work on varying your pace or adding emphasis to certain words. Tape yourself several more times reading the same story and you will be able to see how much you have improved.

Rate of Speech

You don't want to speak too slowly or too quickly. According to authors Glenn, Glenn, and Forman in *Your Voice and Articulation*, most people speak at a rate between 145 and 175 words per minute. If you speak too slowly or pause too often, or if your pauses last too long, your listener will become bored and eventually will tune you out. If you speak too quickly, you might lose your listeners' interest because they have to try too hard to follow what you're saying. Another problem with speaking too quickly is that you might appear nervous, as it is typical to speak faster than normal when you are tense or nervous. If you speak with an accent, be particularly aware that you might not be understood if you speak too quickly. If it appears that your listener does not understand or is confused, the first thing that you should do is speak more slowly.

Exercise: Rate of Speech

If you're interested in discovering your rate of speaking, voice and diction books such as the one mentioned previously have reading passages with time checks. You could also pick a passage from a magazine or newspaper article and count the words, inserting marks to indicate 145, 155, 165, and 175 words. Set a minute timer and read the article at your regular speaking speed. When the timer signals one minute, you'll know your approximate speaking rate.

Volume

You don't want to blast everyone out of the room, but you do want to be heard. Listen to other people during meetings, at work, and at social events. Notice that generally those who speak at a very low volume don't command as much attention as those who speak more loudly. Speak too softly and you may appear timid and unsure of yourself. Speak too loudly and you may appear pushy and aggressive. When presenting or speaking at a meeting, if you are asked more than once to repeat what you've just said, you are not speaking loudly enough. The situation, your location, and even the size of the room may influence your voice volume. For instance, in a crowded room, you may have to speak more loudly than you normally would in order to be heard. The same holds true if you're making a presentation without a microphone. In general, it is wise to aim for a volume that is pleasant to listen to and that showcases you as a confident speaker.

Exercise: Volume

Ask a co-worker to give you feedback on the volume of your voice, both in meetings and throughout the day as you are speaking with other people. Because we might speak more loudly than we think we do, it's helpful to know how others perceive us.

What You Say

What you say involves the actual words that you speak. So, how can you make a good impression with your spoken language? Watch what you say, of course! Every time you open your mouth to speak, consider that your choice of words has an impact on what others think about you. Attention to the following three things will help give you a spoken image that says you are a business professional.

Having a Good Vocabulary

Vocabulary is an important part of your verbal image. Work at having a solid—but not a pompous—vocabulary, one that can truly express your thoughts and ideas. A good vocabulary not only helps when you are the speaker, it will serve you well when you are the listener. You won't have to ask the speaker what he or she means or try to pretend you understand and then hurry to look up a word or two in the dictionary. For example, if your boss says, "That was a good segue," you'll know that he means it was a good transition. You will be able to advance much further in your career if you are able to express yourself well and understand others as they express themselves.

Exercise: Vocabulary

If this is an area you need to develop, there are many tapes and CDs that have vocabulary-building exercises. Purchase a couple of these and listen to them while you are driving, jogging, relaxing, or working out. Be sure that you use your new vocabulary words on a regular basis. If you don't, you'll definitely forget them.

Tempering Disagreement

You might think that being direct is a positive way to express yourself, but be aware that if you are too direct, others might view you as inflexible and closed-minded. For instance, if you are in a meeting and you wish to disagree with a suggestion made by a member of your team, direct remarks such as, "You're wrong!" or "That'll never work!" are too strong. Statements like these will most likely be interpreted as embarrassing "put downs" by the person who made the suggestion, and they also imply that you are totally inflexible. If you soften disagreement, you appear as someone who is able to compromise and find common ground to work toward a solution. Responses such as, "I can see your point on X," coupled with "Have you considered Y?" still indicate disagreement, but make you sound less rigid.

Three words that make disagreement less disagreeable are "would," "could," and "might." Consider the differences between the following direct statements and their tempered counterparts:

Direct: "A meeting on Friday just doesn't work for me."

Tempered: "I already have a meeting scheduled for Friday. Could we schedule our meeting for Tuesday instead?"

Direct: "No one purchases office copiers anymore. Leasing is the only way to go."

Tempered: "Would you consider leasing rather than purchasing the office copiers? I believe it might be more cost-effective."

Speaking Up

Don't be a silent partner. It's important for you to express your opinions and share your ideas. Be sure, however, that you have something valuable to say and that you stay on the subject. Prepare for meetings in advance so that you are able to participate. You don't want to be thought of as too timid or as someone who can't contribute.

What Not to Say

Sometimes what you say can detract from the professional image you want to present. To be sure that your spoken word is businesslike, avoid language that falls into the following categories.

Sexist and Racist Language

These just don't belong in the workplace. First of all, companies are particularly sensitive to language that is considered sexist or racist because of the negative work environment it creates. Secondly, even something supposedly said in jest might be considered the basis for legal action. Finally, if you use either racist or sexist language, you will be viewed as unprofessional by your co-workers and management.

Rambling

When speaking at work, make sure that you stick to the subject. Rambling and going off on unrelated tangents tells others that you have a disorganized thought process. Avoid redundancies for the same reason. (See a list of common redundancies in chapter 2, "Business Writing Basics"). Remember, less is usually more. Think before you speak, taking time to organize your thoughts and weigh your words.

Profanity

What might seem acceptable language to some is not to others. For example, the term "damn" seems quite tame to some, but is very offensive to others. You should never use expletives and vulgarities under any circumstances. There are some words, however, that might not be considered profanity, but are crude or rude. One such word that is used frequently is "suck," as in "That sucks." This word might not be considered profanity in the purest sense, but it certainly has no place in your vocabulary, especially at work. "That bites" or "bite me" are other expressions definitely to stay away from.

Gossiping

The workplace seems to be a fertile breeding ground for this popular but insidious activity. Regardless of its allure, you'll be smart to steer clear of engaging in negative talk about others as well as passing along hearsay. You're probably thinking, "Well, if I'm in a group of people and they begin gossiping about someone, what can I do?" Read the following from a workplace conversation. Which employee would you rather work with?

Dan: "I heard that Kelly is fooling around with David, her boss."

Jennifer: "Really! Well, I guess we now know how she got that promotion last month. I kind of thought there was something between those two. What do you think, Sergey?"

Sergey: "I think I've got a report due Friday, and I'd better get back to it. See you later."

Your presence, even if it's a silent presence, indicates involvement and support of the spread of gossip. Simply excuse yourself by saying something similar to what Sergey said. Besides potentially damaging another person's home life, career, or both, those who gossip are not respected by the people they work with.

Maybe you don't gossip and never have. That's great, but don't fall prey to the temptation to admonish those who are gossiping—especially if one of them is your superior. Most likely, your criticism will fall on deaf ears and you will be labeled as a "holier than thou" type.

Complaining

No one likes a chronic complainer—you know, the person who never has anything positive to say. This person complains about the workload, the boss and co-workers, the office equipment, and so on. He or she is the person that you have lunch with and afterward, instead of feeling refreshed and renewed for an afternoon of work, you feel tired, depressed, and unmotivated for the remainder of the day.

Studies have shown that employers value employees who demonstrate a positive attitude toward their work. One way to do this is to ensure that you don't say negative things that will drain your morale and that of your co-workers.

Conclusion: Image Matters

How you present yourself—how you look, what you say, and how you say it—has a strong impact on your success and advancement in business. Remember that you are being judged on a daily basis by everyone you come in contact with, including your co-workers, managers, and clients. You can make those judgments work in your favor by managing the impression others have of you. If you follow the guidelines given in this chapter and do the recommended exercises, you will be taking important steps toward presenting a professional appearance and feeling confident about your business image.

CHAPTER 2

Business Writing Basics

Business writing. It couldn't be that difficult, right? You've been using e-mail to communicate with your friends and family, and perhaps with your teachers. You've done research and written term papers and reports. But perhaps you're a little nervous about e-mailing a client or submitting a report to your boss. If so, it's probably because you were never offered, or you decided not to take, a business writing class. And because you never studied business writing, you're not quite sure whether you're doing it right. This chapter will give you the basics you need for business writing that is complete and correct, understandable, and easy to read.

In yesterday's business environment, a great deal was communicated through letters. It was a much slower pace back then; people had the time to compose formal business letters, and to send them the snail-mail route. Well, at that time, no other options were available—e-mail had not yet arrived on the scene. Today, we work in a fast-paced business world where more and more, business communication is handled electronically.

Also, the tone of business writing has become simplified—more conversational—not just for e-mail, but for formal business letters as well. People are writing more simply today and the emphasis has shifted to clear, concise communication rather than on impressing the reader—FINALLY! There is a danger, however, in being too casual and conversational. It is still important to be professional and write in a businesslike manner. Today's business communication relies heavily on the written word, but most of the time it comes in the form of e-mail rather than a formal business letter and it is generally read on a screen rather than on letterhead.

The Five *S*'s of Good Business Writing

You can't go wrong if you always aim for writing that is

- Simple
- Suitable
- Sound
- Sufficient
- Succinct

These five writing goals will help you deliver the right message and ensure that your writing is readable, understandable, complete, and correct. Let's look at the five *S*'s that contribute to good writing.

Simple

Writing in a simple manner doesn't mean you are a simpleton—just the opposite. It takes time and effort to simplify a message. The time and effort will be well spent, however, because it will almost always result in writing that is more readable and more understandable.

Your goal is not to impress your reader by using words you think are important sounding; your goal is to communicate information. Why write, "I have perused your report and find…" when you can write, "I have read your report and find…"; or, "The conference will commence with an introduction of the speaker," when you can write, "The conference will begin with an introduction of the speaker." Choose simple words that clearly communicate your point.

Business letters of the past contain many examples of pomposity and wordiness. These letters should be (if they are not already) placed in the company archives and certainly should not be used as samples or templates for current business letters. As early as the 1950s, grammar and writing books identified many old and outdated words and phrases; they advised readers to immediately stop using them. Unfortunately, many business letters still contain outdated language. It's the 21st century, time to retire these older phrases and replace them with updated language that is simple and clear.

Most writing and style books give long laundry lists of out-of-date expressions. Some of the best examples are listed in table 2.1. Take a look and see whether you use any of these. We give alternatives so that you can immediately remove the older terms from your writing vocabulary and begin using the new ones.

Table 2.1: Out-of-Date Expressions

Expression	Example	Replacement
Pursuant to	Pursuant to our telephone conversation of last week…	Regarding our telephone conversation of last week…
Enclosed please find	Enclosed please find the catalog you ordered.	Here is the catalog you ordered. The catalog you ordered is enclosed. I am enclosing the catalog you ordered.
At your earliest convenience	Please send the above documents at your earliest convenience.	Please send the above documents by next Thursday. Please send the above documents by August 15.
In the amount of	Our check in the amount of $50 is enclosed.	Our check for $50 is enclosed. We have enclosed our check for $50.
Under separate cover	The monthly receipts have been sent under separate cover.	The monthly receipts have been sent separately. The monthly receipts are in a separate mailing.
Subsequent to	Subsequent to the feasibility study, we made made major changes to the plan.	After the feasibility study, we made major changes to the plan.
In receipt of	We are in receipt of your payment.	We received your payment.
Please do not hesitate to contact me.	If I may be of further assistance, please do not hesitate to contact me.	If you have any questions, please call.

Suitable

To check that your writing is suitable, you need to ask the following two questions:

1. Does your writing suit the audience?

2. Does your writing suit the purpose?

The following sections will help you determine whether your writing fulfills the preceding two conditions.

Does Your Writing Suit the Audience?

Most likely, the contents of an e-mail to a member of your team wouldn't be the same as one written to a client or someone in top management, even if the subject was the same. Why? Because the latter two people most likely don't need the same type or depth of information. Considering your audience, or reader, is essential to effective business writing.

Put yourself in the reader's shoes so that you are *reader*-focused rather than *writer*-focused. Once something is written and sent, you can't take it back and change it, so make sure that it's suitable before it's sent. Answer the following questions ahead of time for everything you write:

- How much does the reader already know?

- How much does the reader need to know?

- Are you writing with technical acronyms or jargon that your reader might not be acquainted with?

Although your primary audience (the one to whom you are addressing the communication) is the major consideration, remember that there is always the potential for a secondary audience (those who are sent copies by the primary audience). It is impossible to know how far one e-mail might go. You might send an e-mail to a co-worker, who forwards it to his or her supervisor, who forwards it to an executive manager, who makes a hard copy and brings it to a meeting with the CEO. Considering the power of the written word to travel, write to your audience, but be prepared for your writing to end up somewhere you never intended, including in the hands of a client or top company executive.

Does Your Writing Suit the Purpose?

In order to be sure that your writing suits your purpose, you'll need to consider your goal. Do you primarily want to inform, or do you want your reader to take action? Your purpose will guide you and keep you on track as you write.

Second, the organization of your ideas must be suited to a business environment. When writing papers in school, you might have put the most important part at the end, starting out with facts that logically supported and built up to the conclusion. In business writing, it's important to take the most important point or the call to action and put it at the very beginning—in the first sentence or two. You then support that point with facts, and possibly examples. Why is it important to organize your writing this way? Because it is *reader*-focused. Your reader doesn't have the time to wade through the entire e-mail, letter, or report you've written before discovering your point at the very end. Don't put your "bottom line" at the bottom. Your reader wants the "bottom line" up front.

Consider these two examples of a retail department manager's request for additional holiday help. Which one is easier to understand, and which do you think her manager would rather receive?

Yang,

With the holiday season approaching, the jewelry department will be busier than usual. Weekends in fine jewelry and watches, and evenings in costume jewelry, are the times we get the most customers, and we need to address holiday staffing for these three areas.

I have reviewed current employee work schedules and feel that in order to adequately serve our customers' needs, we should hire three part-time, temporary sales associates. I suggest that we have them start December 2.

Best regards,

Melissa

Figure 2.1: Example letter #1.

> Yang,
>
> We are going to need three part-time, temporary sales associates to help out during the holiday season, beginning December 2.
>
> • One person for weekends in fine jewelry
>
> • One person for evenings in costume jewelry
>
> • One person for weekends in watches
>
> Best regards,
>
> Melissa

Figure 2.2: Example letter #2.

Structure your business communications with the "bottom line" at the beginning, as shown in the second example. As you can see, it is easier to understand and takes less time to read.

Third, consider the proper communication tool for your message. You might communicate through a memo, a formal business letter, an e-mail, a fax, or a report. Also available to you are telephone calls and face-to-face encounters. Did you choose the most effective way to communicate? Did you choose the best tool for achieving the desired results? Choosing the most appropriate vehicle for your message might be difficult at times, but it's important to think it through and choose the best means with regard to the message being sent.

E-mail is especially good for day-to-day matters, messages that need to immediately inform, and those requiring immediate answers. However, the use of e-mail is so prevalent in business today that we often forget that there are other ways of communicating with each other, such as in person, by phone, or by letter. Okay, the letter route is a little archaic, but popular as it is, there are times when e-mail should not be used.

One of the times e-mail should not be used is when a sensitive issue needs to be discussed. If you as a supervisor are having problems with an employee who reports to you, you should have a face-to-face meeting with that person.

Aiden's Supervisor Misuses E-mail

When Aiden arrived at work, he opened his e-mail and found a message from his supervisor advising that his performance in the last quarter had not been up to par. The e-mail continued with an admonishment of his lack of commitment to the company; it ended with a notification that he would be given one month to make noticeable improvements in his performance.

Aiden was shocked that his supervisor would e-mail him with this information rather than address his poor performance directly in a face-to-face meeting. Aiden thought that if he were able to meet with his supervisor in person, he would at least be able to respond to the accusations. He would also gain a better understanding of what specific improvements were needed.

A telephone call might be more effective than e-mail, especially when dealing with a disgruntled client. The warmth and sincerity that can be conveyed by the human voice is impossible to convey in e-mail. A phone call or a handwritten note is a good choice for communicating sympathy to a co-worker on the death of a loved one. And, yes, formal letters still have a place in 21st-century business. In fact, there are times when only a formal business letter will do, such as when it serves as a cover letter for a formal business proposal. If your company has a prescribed business-letter format, follow that. Otherwise, see the following guidelines for the structure of a formal business letter.

Company Letterhead

(4–6 line spaces, minimum)

Date

(3–4 line spaces)

Inside Address:

Name, Title, Company, Complete Mailing Address

(2 line spaces)

Subject Line:

Re: The monthly sales reports

(2 line spaces)

Salutation:

Dear Mr./Mrs./Ms., or first name if you know the person well

Follow the salutation with a colon. If using the first name only, it may be followed with a comma.

(2 line spaces)

Body:

Type single space, with two line spaces between paragraphs.

Devote one paragraph to each important point.

(2 line spaces)

Closing:

Sincerely, Yours sincerely, Regards, Best regards, Cordially, or other professional

closing

If two-word closing, only the first word is capitalized.

(4 line spaces, within which your written signature appears)

Signature:

Full name typed.

Below your name, your job title

Never precede a written or typed signature with a title (Mr., Mrs., Ms., Dr.).

(2 line spaces)

Enclosure (if there is one)

cc: (John Doe)

Figure 2.3: A formal business letter template.

Sound

It's important that your writing is sound. Sound writing is correct writing, so check to be sure that your writing is error-free on a variety of levels. Is your grammar perfect? Did you use spell-check? Did you check your spelling using a dictionary, especially with regard to any confusing words? Is the tone appropriate to the message and the audience? Have you checked your punctuation and mechanics?

Confusing Words

In table 2.2, you'll find a listing of confusing words and abbreviations that are often misused in business writing. Read through the list to identify any that give you trouble. Mark this page so that you can easily reference this list and be sure that you are using the correct word or abbreviation.

Table 2.2: Confusing Words and Abbreviations

Words	Explanation
advice	An opinion concerning what could or should be done (noun)
advise	To counsel, suggest, or recommend (verb)
inform	To communicate information or make aware of something
affect	To influence something (verb)
effect	To bring about (verb)
effect	A result or outcome (noun)
among	Use when referring to more than two things
amongst	Interchangeable with among
between	Use when referring to two things
appraise	To determine the value of
apprise	To inform about something
continual	Recurring frequently or on a regular basis
continuous	Uninterrupted
e.g.	Abbreviated from the Latin *exempli gratia*, meaning *for example*
i.e.	Abbreviated from the Latin *id est*, meaning *that is*
its	Possessive form of the pronoun *it*
it's	Contraction for *it is*
farther	More distant, to or at a greater distance
further	At or to a greater extent

(continued)

(continued)

Table 2.2: Confusing Words and Abbreviations

Words	Explanation
principle	Fundamental belief or moral rule (noun)
principal	Main or primary (adjective)
principal	Head of a school (noun)
their	Possessive form of the pronoun *they*
there	A place or point (noun)
	Introduction of clause or sentence (pronoun)
	At, in, or toward that place (adverb)
they're	Contraction for *they are*
weather	Atmospheric conditions with regard to temperature, wind, humidity, and so on
whether	A conjunction used to introduce one alternative or alternative possibilities

Punctuation and Grammar

With regard to punctuation and mechanics, a number of reliable sources are available at your local bookstore or library. It's a good idea to have a reference such as *The Chicago Manual of Style* on hand to refer to for questions concerning punctuation as well as capitalization, abbreviation, numerals, and usage. *The Elements of Style* by William Strunk, Jr., and E.B. White is another good choice, as is *The Associated Press Stylebook and Briefing on Media Law.*

Keep a good dictionary next to your computer so that you can double-check spell-check and to be sure that you are using the proper word. Remember that spell-check is not always your friend. If you wanted to write "if" but instead typed "of," spell-check wouldn't alert you because both are correctly spelled words. Spell-check isn't intelligent enough to know when a word doesn't make sense in a sentence and will miss spelling errors. Look at the following sentences and see whether you can tell what spell-check missed:

1. The mail is usually delivered on the morning.

2. It was there idea to split the work between the two groups.

3. I will read your report tomorrow and got back to you.

4. If its not to late, we'll meet you after work.

Corrections: (1) *in* instead of *on*, (2) *their* instead of *there*, (3) *get* instead of *got*, (4) *it's* instead of *its* and *too* instead of *to*

When proofreading and editing your work, check first for organization, meaning, clarity, audience focus, and tone. Then go back through your document, paying attention to details regarding punctuation, capitalization, abbreviations, and so on.

People will judge you not only by *what* you have written, but by *how well* it is written. Look over your work carefully. If you do, you'll make a positive impression on your readers.

Sufficient

Have you read your writing from the standpoint of your reader? Did you write enough to fully explain? Will your audience understand your meaning so that they don't have to spend the time to ask you to reiterate or clarify?

Give enough information and detail to sufficiently inform, but not so much that your reader begins to doze halfway through what's written. You may have an entire book worth of knowledge about a topic, but that doesn't mean that you have to supply the entire book, especially if all your audience needs is the table of contents!

If you have a diverse audience, it may be difficult to decide just how much information to give. You may be writing a technical report that is geared primarily for technical readers. You need to give this primary audience a great number of details. Your audience, however, may also include a second group of readers, with people in upper-level management who do not need the detail. If so, consider writing a summary of the report for them. Always be alert to the fact that some of your readers might not need—or want—all of the information you are able to supply.

Also, consider your reader's knowledge of acronyms, abbreviations, and business lingo that you routinely use. If there is any doubt that the reader will understand these, you must spell them out the first time you use them. For instance, someone in the airline industry writing to a passenger would not generally use the acronym PNR. If it were necessary to use this acronym for reference, it should be followed by its definition given in parentheses (Passenger Name Record).

When writing an e-mail, include pertinent excerpts of any documents or reports to which you refer so that the reader will be able to review them without having to hunt down the material. If it is not feasible to include excerpts, give detailed information about the section of a document in which the information can be found.

Remember, be sufficient, but not superfluous. Give your readers what they need, and not a bit more.

Succinct

Be concise in your writing, not just in your e-mail, but in any writing you do. Whether it's a proposal, a report, an e-mail, a fax, or a formal business letter, no one wants to read a document that is wordy or one that rambles. Save your readers' time with writing that is focused, organized, and free of wordiness and redundancies.

Active Voice Versus Passive Voice

Your writing will be more concise if you write in the active voice, which is a major reason it is preferred in business writing. In the active voice, the subject of the sentence performs the action. For example, "Ameer wrote the report," is in the active voice because Ameer is performing the action. He is writing the report. This sentence written in the passive is, "The report was written by Ameer." Although the meaning is the same as the first sentence, the subject of the sentence is now report, rather than Ameer. The report is not performing the action.

The passive voice is always wordier than the active voice. Also, active voice is preferred in business today because we want to show that we are taking responsibility for our actions. Consider the difference between, "Your account will be reviewed tomorrow" and "I will review your account tomorrow." In the second sentence, the writer is taking personal responsibility for reviewing the account.

Exercise: Active Voice

Look at the following sentences and label each as "passive" or "active." Then, change any passive sentences to active voice. You'll find the answers at the end of the chapter.

1. _____ The company offers its employees a comprehensive benefit package.

2. _____ Your materials will be delivered this afternoon.

3. _____ The proposal was made by the head of the marketing department.

4. _____ Lisa, Beth, and Sarah were chosen to participate in the focus group.

5. _____ Andy works from his home office most of the time.

6. _____ Our CEO often travels to other countries for business meetings.

Hints for Making Your Writing More Succinct

If you find that you generally give too much information, try doing the following:

1. Decide on the purpose for your writing. Write your purpose on paper and refer to it often as you write. Don't lose sight of your objective. If what you are writing does not support your purpose, you are wandering and need to get back on track.

2. Create a brief outline of the salient points you want to make and stick to it. If you go beyond the outline, check back with your purpose to be sure that the detour is warranted.

3. Put yourself in the reader's shoes. As the reader, ask yourself how much information you would like to have and how much you actually need.

Being wordy can make what we write longer than it has to be. During the editing process is the time to look for phrases or expressions that are wordy or redundant. An extra word here and there can really add up and weigh down your writing. Table 2.3 is a short list of some wordy or redundant expressions with suggestions for making them clear and concise.

Table 2.3: Fixing Wordy Expressions: The Long and Short of It

Wordy or Redundant	Clear and Concise
Adding together	Adding
All of	All
As a result of	Because of
At this point in time	Today, at this time, now
During the time that	During, when
First and foremost	First
In many instances	Often
In the event	If
On account of	Because
Open up	Open

(continued)

(continued)

Table 2.3: Fixing Wordy Expressions: The Long and Short of It

Wordy or Redundant	Clear and Concise
Past experience	Experience
Past history	History
Print out	Print
Refer back to	Refer to

Exercise: Wordiness

Read the following sentences and rewrite them so that they are more clear and concise. You'll find suggested answers at the end of the chapter.

1. I don't know whether or not the first priority should be customer correspondence or weekly reports.

   _____

   _____

   _____

2. The final outcome of our research is that the tests need to be repeated again under more controlled conditions.

   _____

   _____

   _____

3. As a general rule, staff meetings are held on Mondays so that the current status of all projects can be reviewed.

   _____

   _____

   _____

E-mail Writing

Because e-mail is so widely used in business today, let's look at some of the rules that govern this communication. But, first, complete the following exercise to determine what areas you need to work on.

Exercise: Check Your E-mail Abilities

Ask yourself the following questions and place a checkmark next to those that apply to your e-mail writing.

❏ I send or forward jokes, chain letters, religious or inspirational messages, or cartoons to co-workers.

❏ I race through my e-mail, answering as quickly as possible without giving thought to who besides the intended recipient may read it.

❏ I use jargon or acronyms regularly and don't always stop to consider whether my reader is acquainted with them.

❏ I sometimes copy people on my e-mail even though they may not know why they have been copied, or whether an action is expected of them.

❏ I don't always take the time to organize my thoughts and eliminate all excess information before writing.

❏ I sometimes leave the subject line blank. When I do include a subject line, I don't always take the time to make sure it is clear and specific.

❏ I usually use spell-check, but don't also use a dictionary to check my spelling.

❏ I normally don't take time to check my e-mail for grammar and punctuation errors.

❏ Sometimes I don't read my e-mail to check for tone prior to sending.

❏ Readers are sometimes confused by my e-mail and have to e-mail back asking for clarification.

If you checked two or more of the items in the preceding exercise, the following pointers will help you improve your e-mail writing skills and assist you in making your electronic communication more focused, clear, and professional.

If your company has an e-mail policy, you should follow that. Otherwise, this list will help you to send e-mails that reflect the professionalism of both you and your organization.

1. **Include a clear and well-defined subject line.** This helps the reader prioritize e-mail and will help get your message opened promptly. If you need a response by a certain deadline, you might put in the subject line, "please respond by (specific time or date)."

2. **Be clear and concise.** That's the point of e-mail. To be effective, an e-mail should cover one, or at the most two major topics, not a multitude of them.

3. **Keep your message to one screen's length.** If your message is longer than that, you are probably covering too many subjects, being too wordy, or dealing with an issue complex enough to warrant face-to-face or at least voice-to-voice communication.

4. **Write in complete sentences rather than fragments, unless you're using bullet points.** With bullet points, you can use phrases rather than complete sentences.

5. **Don't be too casual in tone.** E-mail is still a business communication, and as such the tone should be professional.

6. **Don't use emoticons, e-mail acronyms, or abbreviations.** Emoticons (smiley faces, and so on) are typically used to indicate emotion. Emoticons don't belong in business writing. For instance, even though you might be elated that your supervisor has approved your vacation, don't include a smiley face in your response to her. Also, don't use unprofessional acronyms and abbreviations such as TTYL (talk to you later) and Plz (please).

7. **Always include a salutation.** For example, start with "Hello Mary," "Good morning," "Good afternoon," or something similar. You should follow the salutation with a comma rather than the customary colon that you'd find in a formal business letter.

8. **Attach a copy of the documents(s) you are referring to in your e-mail, or provide pertinent excerpts.** This saves the reader research time. Also, to assist in viewing e-mail history, most e-mail programs allow you to respond with the previous communication(s) sequenced below the current communication. If this option is available to you, use it. If you don't, you might end up sending or receiving confusing e-mails like the following:

To: Jessie

From: Shabrita

Subject: Your thoughts

I totally agree!

---

9. **Review and edit for spelling, grammar, punctuation, content and tone.** You never know whether your e-mail message will be forwarded, or to whom. It's best to make it well written and error-free.

10. **Don't use e-mail to avoid confrontation or communication that should take place person-to-person.**

11. **Don't copy people who don't need to be copied in an effort to either "cover your rear" or impress upper management.** People receive enough e-mail without receiving ones they don't need. And the primary recipient might feel that you are "tattling" on him or her.

12. **Don't SHOUT by typing in all capital letters.** You can emphasize points by putting them in "quotation marks" or in *italic*.

Remember, you and your organization will be judged not just by the content, but also by the wording, tone, and correctness of your e-mail. Because the quality of your e-mail reflects on your professional image, isn't it worth a little extra time and effort?

Conclusion: Good Writing Is an Essential Work Skill

Your written message communicates much more than what appears on the page or on the computer screen. With everything you write, you send a message about your professionalism, and that of your organization.

You now know how to make your writing work for you rather than against you, and you are acquainted with a variety of potential business writing problems, including use of the passive voice, industry-specific jargon and acronyms, outdated phrases, and redundant expressions. No matter what you write—be it an e-mail, a report, a proposal, or a formal business letter—the things that you have learned in this chapter will help you to write more effectively.

Answers to the Exercises

Active Voice Exercise (Page 44)

1. active
2. passive
3. passive
4. passive
5. active
6. active

Rewrites:

2. The messenger service will deliver your materials this afternoon.
3. The head of the marketing department made the proposal.
4. The human resources manager chose Lisa, Beth, and Sarah to participate in the focus group.

Wordiness Exercise (Page 46)

Suggested rewrites:

1. I don't know whether the priority should be customer correspondence or weekly reports.
2. The result of our research is that the tests need to be repeated under more controlled conditions.
3. Generally, staff meetings are held on Mondays so that the manager can review the status of all projects.

CHAPTER 3 Business Etiquette

Horizontal line separator

How do you spell relief—relief from rude, obnoxious, or insensitive behavior?

M A N N E R S!

Because business etiquette has a strong impact on your ability to succeed in your job, you don't want to be considered discourteous, insensitive, or lacking the basic social graces. In this chapter, you'll find out what you need to know in order to practice good manners, and you may be surprised to learn how easy it can be.

Both inside and outside the workplace, manners do matter because managers and co-workers will observe how you handle yourself. If you want to make a favorable impression, you'll need to be acquainted with today's business etiquette guidelines.

What Is Business Etiquette?

Etiquette isn't static; the rules of etiquette are constantly changing to keep pace with a changing business environment, which includes, among other things, a greater number of women in the workforce. In fact, some of the etiquette rules that were followed 10 years ago are obsolete in today's business world. But, manners themselves never go out of style. Why? Because they contribute to a civilized workplace where people can feel respected and work together in harmony.

There are many misconceptions about etiquette, so let's first define what etiquette is not. It is not about

- Memorizing thousands of rules
- Trying to be someone you're not

- Acting "affected"
- Playing a "know-it-all"

Then, what is etiquette all about? It is

- Respect for others—treating them the way you'd like to be treated; and this goes for employees in all capacities, whether they're found in the mailroom or in the boardroom
- Basic principles governing business activities that show you care about yourself and others
- Poise and confidence, regardless of the business location or situation

What are the advantages to understanding and practicing good business etiquette?

- You'll make a great first impression. You already know that you have only one chance to make a good first impression. Even more importantly, first impressions are lasting; and therefore, you want to make the best impression possible.
- You'll be recognized as an employee who positively reflects the company image.
- You'll feel relaxed at business and business/social events because you'll know what to do and when to do it. You won't have to watch others, hoping to copy their social graces, not knowing whether they really know what they're doing.
- You'll be able to concentrate on the presenter, the conversation, the sale, and so on because you don't have to worry about whether you are doing things correctly.

Check Your Business Manners

Give your business manners a preliminary check by answering "yes" or "no" to the following questions. Then, since people often don't see themselves as others do, ask a trusted co-worker to answer these same questions about you. Be honest with yourself and by all means encourage your co-worker to be sincere in his or her answers. Compare your answers to those of your co-worker. What you learn might surprise you.

1. Do you smile often?
2. Do you have a friendly expression on your face when you're not smiling, or do you perhaps look troubled, distraught, or confused?

3. Is your body language open, or do you give closed signals such as folding your arms across your chest?

4. Do you remember names and use them often when addressing others?

5. Do you actively listen to what others have to say without drifting off, making premature assumptions, or interrupting?

6. Are you prompt for meetings?

7. Do you prepare for meetings?

8. Can you be depended upon to make a deadline?

9. Are you respectful toward management and members of your work team?

10. Are you on time for work and make the most of your time while at work?

11. Do you feel comfortable making introductions at work?

12. Are you confident about your initial greeting, including your handshake?

13. Are you at ease during business luncheons and at business/social events with regard to dining and social etiquette?

14. During conversations, do you avoid gossip at all costs and focus on positive subjects?

Honesty—It's Only Polite

You demonstrate respect for yourself, your co-workers, and your company when you conduct yourself in a sincere and honest manner. Being honest means more than regularly telling the truth; it concerns your actions and behaviors as well as how you handle yourself while at work.

You might think of yourself as honest, but only a truly honest employee could answer all of the following questions with a "yes."

- I have never surfed the Web for personal reasons while at work.

- Everything on my resume is accurate, including the positions held, the dates I worked, and the descriptions of my responsibilities.

- I have never asked a friend to punch in or punch out for me when I arrived late or left early.
- I have never sent personal e-mails from work.
- I have never taken pens, pencils, paper clips, or other office supplies from my company.
- I have never spent time on personal phone calls while at work.
- I have never unnecessarily worked overtime for the express purpose of increasing my income.

After reading through these questions, it's easy to see why employers have identified honesty as an essential employability skill. Employers want employees with character, ones who are trustworthy and dependable. Make sure that your business habits reflect your integrity.

Introductions

Introductions are a critical part of business etiquette. It is everyone's responsibility to introduce people who don't know each other. And, no, forgetting someone's name is not an acceptable reason to avoid making an introduction. If you forget someone's name (and this happens to everyone at one time or another), just admit it. Apologize with a statement such as, "I'm so sorry, I just can't remember your name at the moment." The person you are trying to introduce will supply his name and you can get on with the introduction.

Sometimes you'll find yourself in a situation where there is no one around who can introduce you. At other times, the person who should introduce you does not. In these instances, you'll need to introduce yourself. This is perfectly acceptable.

Sam Bungles an Introduction

Sam was happy that Jim, the new employee, had finally arrived. Sam had been working overtime to cover the job duties of a former team member who had left the company.

As Sam was showing Jim the ropes, a company vice president walked through the department and asked Sam to introduce him to the new employee. Sam stammered, not knowing how to proceed, got tongue tied, and completely bungled the introduction. This could have been an opportunity for Sam to make a favorable impression on upper management; instead, it did just the opposite.

Whose Name Should You Mention First?

Some etiquette books can be confusing with regard to explaining introductions. That's because there is so much talk about who should be introduced to whom. You might ask, "Am I introducing Alan to Beth if I say, 'Alan, I'd like you to meet Beth'? Or, am I actually introducing Beth to Alan when I say it this way?" *Relax.* You don't have to get tied up in the rhetoric. There is a foolproof method that's easy to remember and easy to use.

The first consideration in making an introduction is that the person whose name is mentioned first is the one to whom you wish to show the greatest respect or deference. Know that social and business introductions differ. In social introductions, not only a person's status, but also age and gender are considered (with women and older people being given preference). In business, we are all supposed to be on equal footing, therefore age and gender should not play a role in deciding whose name is mentioned first. What is the deciding factor, then? In business, a person's status, position, or degree of authority is paramount.

When introducing people, say first the name of the person to whom you wish to show the most respect and deference. For instance, if a new employee joins your department and a senior executive stops by, you should introduce them. Do so by saying, "Mr. Senior Executive, I'd like to introduce Ms. New Employee." You have said first the name of the person who should be afforded the most respect—the senior executive. Because gender does not play a role in the workplace, you wouldn't mention the new employee's name first, even though in this instance she is a woman and the executive is a man.

Let's say that a customer is visiting your office. Again, a senior executive strolls by and you wish to introduce them. Start by saying, "Ms. Customer, I'd like you to meet Mr. Senior Executive." That's right. The customer always comes first in business introductions, even when a customer is being introduced to the CEO of the company. Again, notice that gender does not matter. The reason Ms. Customer's name is mentioned first is because she is the customer, not because she is a woman. The same is true for age. It is not a consideration in business introductions.

Provide More Than Just Names

It's important to mention more than names when making an introduction. Let's say that you are introducing Ms. New Employee to Mr. Senior Executive. After the introduction, provide a little more information as a starting point for a possible conversation. You might say in this instance, "Ms. New Employee is our new accounting clerk." And you might add, "Mr. Senior Executive manages our marketing department." That way, each person knows more about the other than simply his or her name.

Exercise: Introductions

Practice the following introductions. Write down what you will say, and then find someone to practice them with. You can find the correct answers at the end of this chapter.

1. Introduce Lori Jones, a fellow employee and Jim Flint, a company manager who is visiting from another location.

   _____

   _____

   _____

2. Introduce Mr. Smith, a customer, and your department manager, Jill James.

   _____

   _____

   _____

3. Introduce your cousin Jean Little, who is joining you for lunch, and your supervisor, John Johns.

   _____

   _____

   _____

Handshakes

Most people choose to shake hands when meeting people for the first time, or when they haven't seen them for a while. Knowing how to shake hands properly can make a great impression on others. Shaking hands improperly can do just the opposite.

Yes, you should shake the hands of both women and men alike. Don't give a wimpy handshake to a woman, thinking that this is what she would prefer. It's not. I have asked a great number of women in my classes and workshops what type of handshake they prefer. The vast majority prefer to receive a firm handshake from both men and women.

Extend your hand and give a warm smile when meeting someone. If you are seated at a table, stand and shake the person's hand. This goes for women as well as men. If the room is very crowded, or you'd have to lean over a wide expanse of table, it is best to just smile and nod in the person's direction, or possibly raise your hand in greeting rather than shake hands.

When you shake hands, give two to three shakes and then break the exchange. You don't want to continue pumping the other person's hand, nor do you want to stop pumping and continue holding the other person's hand. If the other person goes beyond three or four shakes, you should completely relax your grip and move your hand in a downward motion.

If you extend your hand and the other person does not take it, immediately drop your hand to your side, continue smiling, and give an opening statement such as, "It's nice to meet you." There are a variety of reasons why some people dislike shaking hands, including cultural and medical reasons. Be courteous; don't ask why they do not wish to engage in this customary gesture.

Telephone Etiquette

Isn't modern technology wonderful? It can be, if used properly. It can also contribute to or detract from your professional image. The following sections discuss the proper way to communicate using the phone, including voice mail, cell phones, and talking to an actual person.

Your Outgoing Voice-Mail Message

Your company might have a prescribed format for voice-mail messages. If so, follow that format, speaking in a friendly and professional manner. If the voice-mail message content is left up to you, review the following checklist for what it should contain:

1. **A friendly salutation.** Example: "Hello."

2. **Your full name, the day, and the date.** Example: "This is Mary Jones. It is Wednesday, May 23."

3. **The reason the person has gotten your voice mail.** Example: "I am either on the phone or away from my desk," or "I will be out of the office starting May 21, returning May 24."

4. **What options are available to the caller.** Example: "If you need an immediate response, please dial extension 39 and ask for Julie Jeffers, or you may leave a message after the beep." Be sure to notify the caller if your recorder has a time limit. It is frustrating to be cut off in the middle of leaving a voice-mail message. If a person is notified in advance, he or she can shorten the message.

5. **Say thank you.** It is appropriate to say, "I'll return your call as soon as possible." What is not okay is, "I'll return your call at *my* earliest convenience." Remember, the focus should not be on you, but on the person who is calling you. Finally, to end your message, you may wish to add, "Have a great day," or something similar. Since this last line can be cliché, don't add it unless you can sound sincere in your delivery.

Change your voice mail as often as warranted. People sometimes forget to change their messages when they return to the office and the "out of town" message continues on into the week after they have returned. Let's say it's June 16 and you call someone's voice mail and hear a message saying that the person is out of town, but will be back in the office on the 14th of June. You are wondering whether the person has delayed his return, or whether he is indeed in the office but just forgot to update his message. The bottom line is that if you don't consistently update your message, callers may think you are forgetful, inefficient, or disorganized.

It is courteous to return voice-mail calls within 24 hours. If you will be unable to do so, be sure to mention that in your message so that the caller can take advantage of the contact option you have provided.

Leaving a Voice Message

Today, many of us who make business calls speak to recording devices the majority of the time; people in business seem almost impossible to reach by phone. There are many reasons for this, including increased workload, meeting attendance, and business travel. Some busy employees use their voice mail to their advantage by having it screen their calls, thereby allowing them uninterrupted time for paperwork.

Because you will often be speaking to a machine, it's important to be prepared for what to say. Follow these guidelines for flawless phone messages:

1. **Begin with a greeting such as "Good morning," or "Good afternoon (person's name)."** Deliver these words in a friendly, upbeat voice.

2. **Follow the greeting with your identification.** Example: "This is John Jones of ABC Company." If your department or division is of importance, include it.

3. **Briefly state the reason for your call.** Example: "I'm calling to review the sales figures for December with you." Stating the reason for your call allows the person you've called to obtain or review pertinent files, documents, or reports before returning the call.

4. **Provide information regarding times you can be reached.** Example: "I'll be available between 9 and noon and after 3 p.m." Be as specific as possible. When you provide this information, it reduces phone-tag; it also shows that you are considerate of the other person's time.

5. **Repeat your name and give your phone number.** Speak *slowly* and *clearly*. It is extremely frustrating to receive a call and not be able to understand the caller's name or phone number. Pausing after each number in a phone number makes it easier to understand and gives the listener more time to write it down. If you have an accent or speech impediment, it is wise to spell your name. Many a phone call is not returned for the simple reason that the person receiving the message can't understand the name or the phone number.

6. **End the call** with "thank you," "good-bye," "have a good day (person's name)," or another appropriate ending.

Be sure that your message doesn't contain any sensitive or confidential information. A good number of people review their phone messages on speakerphone so that their hands are free to take notes. That means that anyone in the vicinity of the person playing your message might hear its content.

Exercise: Voice Mail

Practice leaving a voice-mail message by leaving one for yourself. You will be able to hear how you sound, including the tone of your voice, your inflection, your speed, and your enunciation. You can use this information to perfect your voice and tone before leaving real messages.

Talking to a Real Person

Sometimes—and this can come as quite a shock—you actually reach a real, live person. Be prepared and know what you will say.

1. Start with a friendly, time-appropriate greeting such as, "Good morning (person's name)."

2. Give your name and company, followed by your division or department, if relevant.

3. State the reason for your call and ask whether it is a good time to talk, giving an indication of how lengthy the call might be. Example: "Joan, is this a good time to talk?" I just need a few minutes to reconfirm the attendees for our conference next week."

Cell Phones

Cell phones have become a ubiquitous part of our lives. Everywhere you turn, you see people engaged in conversations, whether it's in line at the grocery store, driving on the highway, in the hallways at work, on commuter trains, in fine dining establishments—even in movie theaters, churches, and synagogues!

We are so used to having a cell phone at our ears, that we often forget basic courtesies that govern their use. No one wants to hear your personal conversation. If you must speak on your cell phone, go to a location that affords some privacy. If you are at a business luncheon, it's best to put your phone on "vibrate" (if you must be reached); or better yet, turn it off during lunch and retrieve your messages afterward.

Don't bring your cell phone to business meetings or business presentations unless it is absolutely necessary. For instance, if your boss has told you he or she must reach you at a moment's notice, you might wish to explain to other meeting participants that you have left your phone on, and why. If it happens to ring, at least they'll know that it was unavoidable. Remember, though, whenever possible, turn your phone off. There is nothing more distracting than having cell phones ring during meetings and presentations, unless it's people excusing themselves to take a call, and then exiting and reentering the room.

E-mail Etiquette

There are basic principles that govern e-mail writing. The following is a list of e-mail tips:

1. **Be as concise as possible.** You'll indicate to your readers that you are considerate of their time.

2. **Be professional.** Writing in a manner that is too casual might indicate to the reader a lack of respect.

3. **Be sure to include a salutation such as "Good morning Mina," or simply "Mina."** Salutations make e-mail feel more personal and professional.

4. **Use an electronic signature that includes your name, company, title, and phone number.** A reader who wants to respond by phone rather than e-mail will thank you for the courtesy.

5. **Check and respond to e-mail messages regularly** (twice a day if possible).

6. **Don't mark your outgoing e-mail as "urgent" if it is not.**

Because your e-mail manners reflect your professional image, isn't it worth a little extra time and effort to ensure that you are courteous?

You will find more information on how to write effective e-mail messages in chapter 2, "Business Writing Basics."

Cubicle Etiquette

More and more, companies are providing cubicles, rather than offices, for the majority of their employees. Cubicles not only offer the company space savings, they also promote teamwork and improve intra-office communication. Aside from the obvious benefits, there are also the less desirable aspects of cubicles to consider. Life in "cubicle world" can be uncomfortable, and it is often full of pitfalls.

To begin with, cubicles are less spacious than offices, so you must make do with limited space. Management expects employee cubicles to look neat and organized; you never know when a customer might pass through. Never forget that your little home away from home sends a direct message about you and your work habits to management, co-workers, and clients.

Like it or not, the condensed working environment of "cubicle world" seems here to stay. Following are some tips on cubicle courtesies and conduct that will help you keep the peace and make you look good.

1. **Don't use your cubicle as a snack shop.** Some people have drawers full of snacks, candies, fruit, cans of soup—you name it. People around them know who they are because they can hear them contentedly munching away. If you bring a bowl of soup, frozen dinner, or last night's leftovers and eat them at your desk, those around you can't help but notice. Even if what you're eating smells good to you, it might not to others. Sometimes the smell of food can be offensive, especially if it has a strong garlicky or spicy odor. Eat in the cafeteria or lunchroom if your company provides one. If you must eat at your desk, eat something that others can't hear or smell—a sandwich (and not hot pastrami) comes to mind.

2. **Talk softly.** Whether you're on the phone or talking to another person in your cubicle, respect others around you by keeping your voice low. Soundproofed or not, cubicles are not private offices, and it's amazing what can be heard from over and around those padded walls. If someone has just come to chitchat, that conversation is best had at lunchtime or after work. If it can't wait, talk in a public area or even in the restroom. Do whatever you can to avoid being labeled as an idler who spends more time chatting than working.

   If you use a speakerphone, be courteous to the person on the other line as well as those around you by turning down the volume so that only you can hear. Sometimes speakerphones are so loud, anyone passing in the hallway can hear both sides of the conversation. In addition, it is essential that you ask the person on the other end of the line for permission before using the speakerphone option.

3. **Decorate simply.** Like your home or apartment, your cubicle is a reflection of you. Your tastes are represented. So are other telling things, such as how well organized you are, whether you are a pack rat, and whether you are clean and neat. People will judge you by the look of your cubicle. It's best to keep it organized and uncluttered.

Your cubicle is a workspace first and foremost. You needn't display dozens of pictures of your relatives, pets, hobbies, vacations, and so on. A plant is nice if there is room, as are a couple of personal photos, a model car, or a cute little thing you picked up at the flea market. Some people don't have anything personal displayed; their cubicles are drab, lifeless, and sterile. It will make your daily work life more pleasant to have some things around you that make you feel good and that you enjoy. Just don't go overboard.

4. **Respect the privacy of others.** No matter how close the proximity, there is no reason to shout over your cubicle to an associate. Remember that other people will hear you and be distracted from what they are doing. Walk to the nearby cubicle and address the person directly, or simply call him or her on the phone.

If you wish to talk to someone who occupies a cubicle, approach that person's cubicle as if it were an office. If the person is on the phone, come back at another time. If the person is not on the phone, before entering the cubicle ask whether you may speak with her, first giving some idea as to the length of time you'll need. Say, "Do you have five minutes, Nicole? I just need to ask you a quick question," as opposed to "Nicole, do you have some time to talk about the ABC project? I wanted to get your feedback on several issues." It should be obvious that the second encounter will take a considerably longer period of time than the first.

Some people put signs on their cubicles when they don't want to be disturbed. Be sure that you respect those signs. Instead of barging in, you can always leave a voice-mail message or send an e-mail letting the person know that you would like to meet in person, at a time that is mutually convenient.

Exercise: Cubicle Etiquette

You now know that your cubicle communicates quite a bit about you to those around you. Read the description of each cubicle below. Pretend that you are walking by that cubicle and glance in. What would your first impression about its occupant be? Describe the occupant with regard to his or her professionalism and work habits. Is he or she the friendly, hardworking, organized person you'd like to see on your team? Would you use words like "attentive to detail," "efficient," "friendly," and "motivated," or others like "lazy," "disorganized," "sloppy," or "aloof?"

Description of Cubicle	Impression of Occupant
Cubicle is cluttered. Papers, files, and folders are stacked in piles on the desk and on the floor. Drawers can't close because they are jammed with papers.	
Cubicle regularly has "Do Not Disturb" signs posted and yellow crime scene tape strung across the doorway. The screen saver on the computer has a "Keep Out" message.	
Cubicle looks orderly. Papers on desk are stacked neatly, overhead storage areas are organized, and there are no files on the floor.	
Cubicle looks very congested. The desk is overflowing with pictures of the kids, the pets, and the last few vacations, along with colorful souvenirs and knickknacks.	
Cubicle looks like a good place to visit if you're hungry. Broken chips, stray nuts and errant pieces of popcorn and candy can be found on the desktop as well as on the chairs and the floor.	

Meeting Manners

Undoubtedly, you will find yourself invited to and your attendance expected at a number of meetings. How you conduct yourself tells all other attendees—including influential management types—about your professionalism. Here are some guidelines to help you make a great impression:

1. **Be on time.** Regardless of how you were notified of the meeting, make a note of it on your calendar and check your calendar daily. Make sure that you are on time for the meeting. Don't allow yourself to be waylaid by a co-worker or engaged in what could be a lengthy phone conversation just prior to the scheduled meeting time. As important as it is to be on time, it is also important not to arrive at a meeting too early because this may indicate one or both of the following: 1) You are too eager. 2) You aren't busy and have nothing better to do. But neither do you want to be late. Being late sends the message that you are self-involved, disorganized, and disrespectful of other people's time.

   It's best to arrive at the proposed time or just a few minutes ahead of time. If you have to travel to a meeting and you are early, drive around or stop for a cup of coffee instead of spending the extra time in the reception area.

2. **Be prepared.** If you have been given an agenda, go over it thoroughly to acquaint yourself with what is proposed to be covered. If you did not receive an agenda, call or e-mail the person who called the meeting to ask what will be covered. Consider in advance how you might be involved in what will be discussed and what you might need to review or bring to the meeting in order to appear on top of things. Also think about what contributions you might be able to make on the proposed topics.

Lynn's First Business Meeting

Lynn was excited. She had started her job at the company just two weeks ago and her boss had enough confidence in her to ask her to attend a client meeting. Lynn made sure that she was early, and finding the conference room open, took a seat at the head of the table. She got comfortable and waited 15 minutes until the scheduled meeting time.

(continued)

(continued)

Later, when her boss arrived with the client and other co-workers, he advised Lynn that she was in his seat and would need to move. Later, Lynn's boss advised her that there were some last-minute meeting preparations that he needed help with but that he had been unable to find Lynn. Never having attended a business meeting, Lynn had no idea that the seat at the head of the table is generally reserved for the chairperson, nor did she know that it is not wise to arrive at a meeting too early.

3. **Be aware of seating significance.** If this is the first time you have attended this type of meeting or the meeting is at a location outside your company, such as a client's office, take your lead from others or simply ask whether there is a specific seat you should take.

   If the number of chairs at the conference table is too few to accommodate everyone, usually a second row of seats is added along one or both walls. Try to obtain a seat at the table. Being seated along the wall puts you in a secondary position and makes it difficult for you to be visible, to be recognized, and to contribute to the proceedings.

   Never take the chair at the head of the table unless you are chairing the meeting, and be aware that the seat to the right of the chair is often reserved for a client, a guest, or for the chair's assistant. Do try to sit as close to the chairperson as possible without occupying another's regular seat.

4. **Manage yourself and your possessions.** Body language speaks loudly about you. Check your posture as you enter the meeting. The first impression you give should be one of confidence, so stand tall. During the meeting, check to be sure that you are not slouching in your seat, or you'll give the impression that you are either bored or self-conscious. Looking too casual with an arm slung over the back of the chair or your hands folded behind your head also sends the wrong message—that you are cocky or overconfident. Keep your elbows off the table, but forearms are okay, especially if you are taking notes. Otherwise, it's best to keep your hands in your lap.

   Purses, briefcases, and other personal paraphernalia should be stored on the floor, out of sight. A tablet of paper, portfolio, appropriate files, and notes are acceptable, but keep the area in front of you neat and tidy. Frantically flipping through your papers and notes to find what you're looking for tells others that you are disorganized.

Business/Social Etiquette

Sometimes the line between our business lives and our social lives blurs. We may be invited to a company outing, a holiday party, or lunch with a client. It is important to remember in these instances that although the event might be labeled social, the underlying reason you are there is for business. There is not a more important time than the business/social event to present a professional image. Many a career has been ruined at the proverbial "office Christmas party." Make sure yours is not one of them.

How to Dress

There are several things you should pay particular attention to with regard to business/social events. The first is dress. Make sure that you are dressed appropriately for the occasion, time of day, and accepted local style. You certainly wouldn't wear a sport coat to a golf outing. Neither should you wear khakis and a polo shirt to a black-tie affair. A party given at the boss's house might not be as dressy as one given at a four-star hotel. Also, appropriate dress for similar social events might differ, based on the part of the country in which they are held. You may notice that in small or rural towns, dress tends to be more casual than in large, cosmopolitan cities.

If dress suggestions are not given on the invitation, it is appropriate to ask what is acceptable. Most of the time you can find out from co-workers, especially those who might have previously attended a similar event.

One thing is sure—suggestive attire is *never* appropriate, whether it's wearing a revealing halter top to a company-sponsored ballgame or a clingy décolletage gown to a formal affair. Don't forget that you send a powerful message through your choice of clothing. That message tells others what you think about yourself. If you wish to be viewed as a competent professional, dress as one. When in doubt, it is best to take clothing cues from respected co-workers and managers at your company.

How to Act

Another thing to be aware of is adherence to social niceties, including introductions and handshakes. These were covered earlier in this chapter. Remember that because "after hours" or "out-of-office" social events are primarily business, business rules govern introductions.

Food is served at many social events; therefore knowledge of proper dining etiquette is essential. If your table manners are rusty, give them a brush up. If you never had good table manners, get some. There are many excellent etiquette books available at your local library or bookstore. Or, you may wish to attend an etiquette class given at a local community college. The time you spend will be worthwhile. You will appear confident and feel at ease. Instead of stressing out about whether you're using the correct utensil, you can concentrate on more important things, such as having a meaningful conversation with your client or boss.

Cocktail parties and buffets offer their own challenges. You might find yourself juggling an appetizer plate and your drink while trying to greet and shake hands with others. It is always a good idea to position yourself near a table so that you can put down the glass or plate in order to shake hands. If you are circulating and have a drink in hand, put the drink in your left hand so that your right hand is free to shake hands. And, keep a supply of business cards in your pocket or purse in case you are asked for one.

In addition to food, alcoholic beverages are often served at social events. It is best not to drink at all, but if you must, have one cocktail or glass of wine and "nurse" it. Drinking alcoholic beverages is never expected, and you don't need to feel pressured into drinking just because others are. If other people overindulge and make complete idiots of themselves, better them than you.

Conclusion: Etiquette Plays a Part in Your Success

This chapter has acquainted you with the basics of business etiquette, from making introductions, to leaving a voice-mail message, to conducting yourself properly at business/social events. Because every company has its own written and unwritten protocol, it is wise to be observant and follow the lead of those in upper management at your organization.

There is no doubt that being courteous and considerate and consistently practicing good business etiquette has a lot to do with career success. Contribute to your success by practicing what you have learned in this chapter.

Answers to the Exercise (Page 56)

1. **Lori Jones and Jim Flint:** "Jim, I'd like to introduce Lori Jones. Lori works with me in human resources. Lori, this is Jim Flint. He's the head of production at our Rockford plant."

2. **Mr. Smith and Jill James:** "Mr. Smith, I'd like you to meet Jill James, our operations manager. Jill, Mr. Smith is the financial officer from XYZ Company."

3. **Jean Little and John Johns:** "John, may I introduce my cousin Jean Little. Jean, this is John Johns, my supervisor and a vice president of the company." You may wish to add additional information such as, "Jean is visiting from Omaha and is joining me for lunch today."

PART 2

Working with People

CHAPTER 4 Dealing with Difficult Co-workers

L ife outside of work is wonderful because you can choose the people with whom you associate and you can avoid those people with whom you don't want to associate. You seek out the company of people who are like you, or who will help you grow in some way. You spend time with people who make you laugh, or love you, or act in some other way that is of value to you. Unfortunately, we don't have these kinds of choices when it comes to the people with whom we work.

More and more people are saying that work wouldn't be so bad if they didn't have to put up with the people with whom they worked. Still, everyone needs to realize and accept the fact that we do not have to like the people we work with, but we do have to develop effective ways of working with others.

Six Basics for Dealing with Difficult Co-workers

The six most important things to remember, regardless of the nature of the difficult co-worker, are

1. **Don't take it personally.** In most situations, they are not lashing out at you specifically. It's just that you happen to be in the wrong place at the wrong time and end up getting the brunt of their temperament-of-the-moment. They simply want someone to lash out at to relieve some of their stress and frustration, and you become the convenient—rather than intentional—victim.

2. **Getting upset will get you nowhere.** With some people, it will only get you more of the same because they have found out that you're vulnerable to their whims. For example, if a person finds one of your "hot buttons" and you react (giving them some kind of cheap thrill), they will continue to push your "hot button" just to get the response.

3. **Whenever possible, look for the humor in every situation.** That doesn't mean laughing at the people involved; it means learning to look at the situation from a humorous perspective to save your own sanity. That's not always easy to do; however, time and distance from the situation do help!

4. **Look for the positive in every situation.** At the very least, you can learn from each of the difficult co-workers how *not* to behave in a work environment if you want to be successful. Another twist on this is that when the difficult co-worker complains about another employee, share your positive experiences with that person. For example, "That's really interesting. Whenever I've had to work with Joe, he's always gone out of his way to be friendly and helpful."

5. **Some people truly do not realize their behavior is irritating to others.** There are those who believe that their behavior falls within the "normal" and acceptable realm of work behaviors. Of course, there are also those who know their behavior is out of line and either simply don't care or have rationalized it.

6. **Stay out of the situation if it does not have a direct, negative impact on you.** Your job (unless it is that of a social worker, counselor, or similar mental-health professional) is not to improve the work behavior of others in a broad, general sense. It is, however, your responsibility to address those situations that directly impact your ability to perform your job competently. If a person's behavior is interfering with that, then—and only then—should you even think about talking to the person about it.

Profiles of Difficult Co-workers You Might Encounter

In an ideal world, we would be able to avoid working with difficult co-workers—or there simply wouldn't be any. Unfortunately, the ideal world doesn't exist. So, without further ado, let's look at 13 different co-workers who can severely challenge your ability to function effectively without the use of Prozac.

Fragile Francis

Francis is a very sensitive person, and the slightest thing said to her, if she misconstrues it (and she's highly likely to do that), causes her to fall apart. She has a tendency to take very innocuous statements the wrong way. When you say, "What's this? Leaving after only 10 hours?" to her as she's walking out, she thinks that you're criticizing her and questioning her work ethic. When pushed too often or too far, Fragile Francis becomes negative—and potentially explosive. She's likely to say things like, "How dare you question my work ethic?" or "I work harder than 90 percent of the people around here. I wonder how they'd like it if I just played around like everyone else."

> **Risky:** "Wow it's only 6:30. Going for the early quit again today, I see!"
>
> **Better:** "Wow, 6:30! I'm glad to see that you're getting out of here a little earlier tonight. You deserve it!"

When dealing with a Fragile Francis, choose your words carefully. Recognize that there are some people you can joke around with and make dry, sarcastic remarks to who will understand that they are said in humor; and there are those with whom you cannot use this approach.

If Fragile Francis has done something about which you need to give some constructive feedback, make sure that you focus on the issue, not on her. The key here is providing constructive feedback, not criticizing her. Your goal should be to present the constructive feedback in such a way that she doesn't feel that she is personally under attack.

> **Risky:** "You really pissed me off in that meeting this morning. What gives you the right to call one of my ideas stupid? You don't always come up with the absolute best ideas all the time."
>
> **Better:** "In the meeting this morning when you said that my idea was stupid, I felt like we were working against each other rather than on the same team. Help me understand where you were coming from on your comment."

Slacker Steve

Steve is the co-worker who doesn't take his job seriously, thereby making yours more difficult. He's never met a task or project that can't wait. It's not that he can't do his job; it's that he simply doesn't want to do it. His motto is, "If I don't do it...someone else will." If Steve applied half the energy he devoted to avoiding work to actually doing it, he'd be a star performer.

Nothing is more important to Steve than the ability to call his friends to make after-work plans and to chit-chat. He's not a happy person when someone interrupts his personal life to ask that he do some work.

You have to give Steve credit, though. He does have a talent—a talent for knowing just how far he can push his do-nothing behavior. He has become incredibly skilled at walking the fine line between keeping his job and getting fired.

So, being a good team member, you grit your teeth, pick up the slack that Steve has caused, and never say a word to anyone, particularly the boss. What does that get you? Longer hours and more frustration.

Deal with Steve by letting him sink or swim. If he has agreed to get something done by a certain date or time, let him be responsible. If he doesn't do it, he will need to explain his behavior to the rest of the team and the boss. Although this might not immediately get results, eventually Steve's performance will be noted and, hopefully, corrected; or he'll be terminated.

Wise Willi

Wise Willi is the intellectual of the group. Although it is great having someone on the team with a wide array of knowledge, it can also be irritating. Sometimes Willi will feel insulted if his ideas, comments, directives, or other contributions are questioned in any way. Even an innocent, "Really? I didn't know that!" could send Willi into an irrational tailspin. (He rationalizes his explosion with thoughts like, "How stupid can one person be? Any idiot with half a brain would know that!" or "I don't know how much longer my patience is going to last if I have to keep dealing with these idiots!")

Overruling Wise Willi can make you feel like choosing death would have been a happier option. When Willi doesn't get his way, he has a range of ways he might react. He might become sarcastic, loud, and hyper-critical. Alternatively, he might become withdrawn and sulky, punctuating what is going on with heavy sighs, shaking his head, snickering, and other nonverbal and semiverbal mannerisms. However he does it, Willi typically tries to make it so uncomfortable for everyone that co-workers often change their minds and decide to do what he wants just to stop his disruptive behavior.

> "Willi, what would happen if we did *A* like you are suggesting and also did *B*?"
>
> "You can answer this question better than most, Willi. How can we combine *A* and *B* to improve the quality of the solution and get everyone's buy-in?"

There are a couple of ways of dealing with Wise Willi. One of the things he wants is respect for his extensive expertise and knowledge. When Willi rears his ugly head during a meeting, comments that provide that respect are most likely to get him to back down. For example:

> "I know you're an expert on this and I respect that; but, I thought the decision was supposed to be made by the group after weighing all alternatives."
>
> "You might be right. But isn't the point of this discussion to help all of us who are newer learn?"

Avoid telling Willi that his plan won't work or that his idea isn't the best. It will only result in him becoming increasingly defensive or turning into an obnoxious bully. Instead, ask him questions for additional information. Probing questions and "what if" questions will help him "discover" problems with his ideas or alternate proposals on his own.

Another technique that is effective—and can help you grow and develop—is to tap into Willi's knowledge and expertise. Wise Willi likes nothing more than showing off his knowledge and expertise, so give him the opportunity to do so—either within a restricted timeframe or outside of the meeting (offline).

> **Offline:** "That's all new to me. After the meeting, can we take about 15 minutes and you can tell me more about that?"
>
> **Restricted timeframe:** "I don't think most of us are familiar with that. Would it be OK with everyone if we take five minutes and have Willi tell us a little more about that?"

Glenda the Gossip

There's nothing Glenda the Gossip likes more than a good piece of gossip. Glenda, at her worst, embellishes what she hears—because it's not quite spicy enough—and then passes it on to half a dozen (or more) people. Her favorite song? *I Heard It Through the Grapevine,* of course. If she only worked as hard at her job as she does on finding out the latest gossip on senior management, what other people are earning, who is dating whom, and all the other little tidbits floating around, she'd be a great team member. Glenda tends not to linger in anyone's office beyond passing on gossip and gathering any new gossip. Her goal is to gather and disseminate as much juicy gossip as possible in an 8-hour day.

How much of a problem is Glenda? A 2001 poll commissioned by WordsCanHeal.org showed that an incredible number of people—51 million—are hurt by gossip each week. Seventy-nine percent of the poll respondents said that gossiping about other people is a problem in the workplace.

Although the temptation is great, don't always write off what Glenda is saying as malicious rumors. Sometimes, she can provide valuable information relative to organizational politics and management preferences. When she finds out that you have a meeting with Kurt, she may well say, "Double-check your work before you go in to meet with him. He's a stickler for the details. I remember Donna telling me about a meeting she had with him...." The first part of Glenda's monologue gives you great information on preparing for your meeting. The second part may be a real-life example, but it also may be nothing more than unfounded rumors.

If you find out that she is simply gossiping, and you'd rather not hear it, let Glenda know that you're not interested. As long as you allow her to prattle on about the latest gossip, she is going to assume that you are a willing listener and keep you on her gossip-spreading list.

> **Glenda:** "Did you hear that Sue—the new manager in accounting—has been cozying up to our executive vice president?"
>
> **You:** "Glenda, I really don't get into talking about that kind of stuff. And I have a lot of things I need to get done. So, if you'll excuse me."

You can also deal with Glenda by focusing on the facts. Too often, the facts are minimal in gossip—otherwise it wouldn't be juicy gossip. If you consistently challenge Glenda on the factual basis of what she is saying, she is likely to avoid bringing the gossip to you.

> "Have you checked with _____ to make sure that's true?"
>
> "Who told you that?"
>
> "Who can tell us whether this is true or not?"

You also need to look at your culpability in the world of gossip. Are you sharing information with others that could be considered gossip, but not calling it gossip (that is, what you are saying is not verifiable fact)? Continue to contribute at your own risk. Not only will it keep you in the circle of gossip sharers, but you may also find that your "innocent speculation" turns into a rumor down the road and damages your reputation.

Also, be aware that if Glenda is gossiping about others, she is likely talking about you behind your back, too. Although the temptation is to strike back with a little gossip of your own, all you're going to do is start a feud you can't win and it will likely end up damaging your reputation. You have two choices on handling this aspect of Glenda. One is that you can simply ignore what is being said, realizing that those who know you well are not likely to believe the gossip. Hopefully, in this case, the gossip will die a natural death or someone else will stop Glenda. Alternatively, you can try to talk to Glenda in a nonthreatening way that lets her know that you are aware of what is going on.

> "I just heard the most amazing thing, Glenda, and thought you ought to know about it. I was told that you were spreading a rumor about me that I _____. I'm sure you wouldn't say anything like that because you know it's not true. I just wanted to let you know this is happening. I told the person who told me about it that I was sure you didn't really say that. So, I've been able to stop at least one person from spreading that lie about you."

Sherman the Tank

Sherman is always right, even when he's wrong. It's a throwback to the old-style "my way or the highway" manager, but in co-worker form. When you walk into a meeting and see Sherman, your heart sinks, your stomach knots up, your mouth feels like it's stuffed with cotton, and you groan internally. It's not because of that pastrami on rye you had for lunch—it's because you know that if Sherman doesn't get his way—right or wrong—he's going to make everyone's life miserable. Unlike Wise Willi, Sherman isn't necessarily an intelligent person—even though he considers himself to be Mensa material. He truly believes that his brilliance should be shared and freely lets people know what he believes is best for everyone and everything.

He's often described as pig-headed, stubborn, and a bully. He sees everything as a battle to be won. He doesn't care whose feelings are hurt ("So-and-so is just too sensitive") or whose toes he steps on ("If he was doing something instead of standing in the way, I wouldn't have had to step on his toes"). Sherman has been known to "win" by threats, intimidation, and downright obnoxious behavior.

> "I understand your perspective, Sherman. But every situation can be looked at from a number of different perspectives. It's our responsibility to come up with the best solution and that means looking at all perspectives. Now, let's get back to...."

Sometimes it feels like it would be easier to just do it his way—even though it's not the best way—rather than put up with his tirade. Although the temptation is to buckle under Sherman's pressure, hold your ground. Be firm, but persistent, in discussing the issue from all perspectives when it is not Sherman's decision to make.

Also, recognize that Sherman's approach could well be considered harassment. Most companies have policies against harassment. If there is an issue of harassment—if you feel you are being harassed—let Sherman know that you find his behavior harassing and if it doesn't stop, you will report it to management. Although that will wake up most Shermans, be prepared for him to respond with a sarcastic or rude comment ("Waah. Little baby can't fight his own fights? Have to go to mommy in management? What a wimp!"). Sherman is trying to bait you. Don't take the bait.

Watching your emotional level may be the trickiest part in dealing with Sherman. It is not unusual, when someone is yelling at you, to yell back. The only thing that happens then is that the situation is escalated and nothing productive occurs. Instead, maintain eye contact with Sherman; take slow, deep breaths; and calmly listen to what he has to say—without responding. When he is finished, clearly and succinctly summarize what he has said, and state your case or your intended action.

> "Your opinion is ____. I understand that. Please understand that I disagree because ____. At this point, I think the most appropriate action to take is ____. Which is what I am going to do."

Not-My-Job Nelly

You don't have to talk to Not-My-Job Nelly to know her—she's the one standing there pointing the finger of responsibility at everyone except herself. "That's not *my* job" or "that's not in *my* job description" is her mantra. Don't even bother to point out that in everyone's job description it says, "All other duties as assigned" because she will find a "logical" reason why that duty should not be assigned to her.

To deal with Nelly, try starting with your version of "we're all part of the team and need to work together to get things done and be successful." Don't be surprised, though, if Nelly feels that she is working as part of the team—even doing more than her fair share of the work. If that is the approach she takes, there is nothing you can do to convince her otherwise.

As her co-worker, you can't directly do anything about Nelly. So don't let her upset or irritate you. Focus on what you can do something about. You *can* form support alliances with your other co-workers. Focus on the rest of you supporting each other and helping each other out and don't worry about Nelly. It might take a while, but Nelly's lack of teamwork will catch up with her and will be resolved—one way or the other.

Best Buddy Bob

Best Buddy Bob wants to share with you the graphic details of his life—things you don't want to know about yourself, much less about a co-worker. He sees the office as part of his extended family. After all, he figures, he spends enough time with everyone at the office to consider them family. The worst part about Bob is that he often expects you to bare your soul to the extent he has bared his. Sometimes he even (horror of horrors) asks for your advice on very personal, intimate topics.

Despite what Bob says, there is nothing wrong with the fact that you feel uncomfortable hearing—and talking about—these kinds of things. You have a right not to have to listen to someone else's personal life issues, particularly in a work environment. You don't have to answer his questions, comment on his exploits, or give him personal advice. The best approach is to tell him you're not interested in hearing what he has to say just as soon as he starts his revelation.

There is also the issue of harassment to consider, whether Bob is of the same or opposite gender. Be firm with him in letting him know that you do not want to hear, and do not appreciate hearing, about the personal aspects of his life. If he persists in sharing intimate details with you, let him know that what he is doing is inappropriate and unwelcome, and if it happens again you will report the situation to human resources.

Negative Nancy

Call Negative Nancy what you want: a pessimist, Chicken Little, a wet blanket, or a cynic. It all boils down to Nancy being the employee who sees the world—or at least the world as she has come to know and expect—to be coming to an end sometime within the next few seconds. If there is any chance of anything going wrong, Nancy will not only be able to precisely pinpoint it, she will be able to dwell on it *ad nauseam*. Her mantra is "That'll never work."

Since Nancy is likely to start her doleful predictions before the problem has even been fully defined, the first thing you want to do is to get Nancy to simply suspend judgment for a few minutes so that everyone can agree on the definition of the issue or problem.

> "Nancy, let's first just come to agreement on what the problem/issue is. Then we'll know how bad the situation is and where to start working on it."

Your next challenge will be to get her to suspend her dire predictions and woeful moaning during brainstorming. One of the best ways to do this is to start out a session by reviewing your group's rules for brainstorming, which probably don't allow for negative critiques of others' ideas. Even if you're not in charge of the meeting, you can still say, "Before we start brainstorming, can we all take a minute and review the rules of brainstorming." Then when Nancy starts breaking the brainstorming rules, it's relatively easy to point out the ground rules to her.

Nancy tends to irritate most people during meetings when she can find nothing right with any suggestion. The reality is that this is one of the times that you can actually tap into Nancy as an expert—use her as the "devil's advocate." The whole idea of coming up with a solution to a problem is to stop the problem from happening again. Because Nancy is an expert at finding holes in solutions, let her find the holes so that they can be plugged *before* you proceed.

> "Nancy, you always do a good job of figuring out where potential solutions can go wrong. How about taking a try on this one. What could go wrong with this solution?"
>
> "We really could use a devil's advocate on this one. Nancy, would you get us started looking at the potential problems with this solution?"
>
> **One on one:** "Nancy, I need help. I think there are some problems with this plan, but I just can't figure them out. Would you take a look at it and see what you think?"

The important thing to remember with Nancy is that she sees no alternatives—she just knows that what you think, what you want to do, what you are proposing, and so on won't work. And that is one of the keys to dealing with her.

When Nancy says "it won't work" don't bother to argue with her. She will criticize anything until the sun goes down, but rarely has a constructive, workable alternative to propose. Let her know that you want to take her specific examples and experiences into consideration, but unless she can come up with something specific, you need to proceed. In most situations, when Nancy is pressed for specifics, she comes up empty. Her goal is not to get you to do what she wants (like Sherman the Tank); it's simply to nix everything with her unproductive criticism. When you focus on the specific "why" of her objectives and she can't provide it, she will eventually give up this behavior with you.

> **Nancy:** "It's not going to work."
>
> **You:** "Specifically, why won't it work?"
>
> **Nancy:** "It's just not gonna."
>
> **You:** "Nancy, I want this to be successful. If you can give me specific information on why this won't work, we can plug up the holes so it will work.

(continued)

(continued)

Nancy: "You'll just have to trust me on this one. I've been around a few more years than you have and I just know these things."

You: "Nancy, I want to take your experience into consideration. If you can give me specifics, I'll be able to do that. If you can't, I'm just going to have to go with my plan as it is."

Too often Nancy is allowed to become a contagion, slowly eroding individual and team morale. Recognize that the team allows her to do that; she doesn't have the power to do it on her own. On a one-on-one basis, choose when to interact with her, when not to, and when to cut your losses and get out of a conversation with her. It's not her fault she's getting you down. She's only responsible for herself, as you are for yourself.

Betty Blamer

Betty Blamer never does anything wrong. Everything that goes wrong in her life is the result of something or someone else. You have to admit, though, she can come up with some pretty creative excuses:

- "I would have gotten it done on time, but the sun was shining on my computer screen and it blinded me."
- "I didn't say I'd do that. Greg suggested me, but I never agreed to do it!"
- "I tried to get it done, but our departmental copier was broken this morning."
- "Don't blame me. I tried to get it done, it's just that Jeff didn't get me the information I needed. I asked him for it quite a while ago. So, it's really his fault it's not done."
- "What do you mean you e-mailed me about that? You should never e-mail something that important. You should have come to my cube and talked to me about it!"

There is absolutely nothing that Betty has ever done or will ever do wrong. Her heart is pure. It's just that circumstances and people—beyond her control—keep getting in the way of her doing what she's supposed to do.

"Betty, you did ask me if I would be able to download the data when you needed it. I told you to let me know exactly what you needed at least three days before you needed it. I never heard back from you. If you'll tell me right now what you need, I can have it to you by the end of the day tomorrow at the latest."

It's very difficult to deal with Betty from a peer standpoint. When she points the blame toward you—and you are absolutely certain it was not your fault—you can be specific as to what you did and didn't do, but don't get into an argument with her. You won't win, and you'll end up looking like *you* are to blame.

When she comes to you to point the finger at someone else, resist the urge to comment on the situation in any way. She is trying to put you in the middle of something you shouldn't even be involved in. Tell Betty firmly, clearly, and specifically to discuss and resolve the situation with the person with whom she has the problem. Then go back to your own work. Don't allow Betty the opportunity to "But..." you back into the situation.

> "Betty, I don't know anything about what you and Mark worked out. If you think he's doing something that's making it impossible for you to do what you need to do, you need to tell him and work it out together."

Status Quo Stan

To say that Status Quo Stan likes things the way they are is an understatement—he will actually do whatever he can (as far underground as possible, of course) to stop any kind of change from occurring. If you've read *Who Moved My Cheese,* he is the personification of Hem (or even, initially, Haw). Most people who end up being a Stan have had either a very significant negative experience with change or a series of small negative experiences with change.

Stan comes in two varieties. One is the verbal Stan who makes it clear that "Nothing good can come of this. You all remember what a disaster it was when they did _____, don't you?" or "There's nothing wrong with the way we've been doing it for years. I don't know why someone has to go and try to screw things up."

The other is the back-door subversive Stan who outwardly appears to be accepting of the changes, if not actively championing them. In reality, he is either actively working behind the scenes to do what he can to sabotage the change effort or simply has no plans to implement the change.

Recognize that whichever Stan you're dealing with, what he's feeling is not uncommon. People resist change for many reasons including that they

- Are afraid that they won't be able to be successful in the changed environment or will make mistakes that will cause them to look foolish

- Do not understand the benefits of the new system/process/procedure

- Are afraid that the change is just going to mean more work for them

- See the change as being inconsistent with their values and/or beliefs

- Do not see a place for them in the changed environment, culture, or system

Although the organization and Stan's manager are supposed to provide—to all employees—the information employees need to be successful through any change process, this doesn't always happen. When you have as little information as Stan does, it's hard to be of too much help sometimes. You can, however, do the following:

- Become a role model.

> "I felt the same way you did at first. I realized, though, that if I got involved in the change, I could have some say in what happened and make it a whole lot easier on myself."

- Share what you know to be facts about the change or question the authenticity of the "facts" the person is sharing with you.

> "I know. I heard the same rumor. The reality is—and I heard this from [major player in the change or someone in the know] that the reality is _____."

- Share what you know to be the benefits of supporting the change.

> "I wondered why we had to go through this, too. So, I did a little research and found that a lot of other companies have done the same thing. And they all had the same benefits: [specify benefits]."

Chatty Cathy

Chatty Cathy, motor mouth, blabbermouth, windbag, chatter box—whatever you want to call her, she talks incessantly. Sometimes Cathy starts off with legitimate business and then strays into unimportant, non-work-related chit-chat so that it takes a crowbar to get her out of your workspace. Sometimes, though, she just wanders in, plops down, and talks—and talks, and talks....

Unlike Glenda the Gossip, Cathy generally doesn't care what she talks about as long as she's not working. In Cathy's philosophy, she sees herself as taking the first step in building an effective team. After all, she reasons, the more you know about your co-workers, the better working relationships you can build with them. And what better way to build a team, she rationalizes, than sharing information with you about other people in the company; her perspective on what is going on in the company, department, and team; her views on the global economy and its impact on the price of tea in China; and all sorts of other topics that are of absolutely no interest to you.

There are a variety of options on how you can deal with Cathy, depending on your style, your work environment, and Cathy's unique approach to chatting.

1. The least offensive approach—but also probably the one Cathy is least likely to recognize—is to send nonverbal messages that you are not interested in chatting. For example, when Cathy walks in, don't make eye contact with her.

2. Use "closed" responses that let Cathy know you are not interested in gossiping. When you fail to "invite" her continued talking by asking questions and acting surprised or interested, part of the thrill of talking with you goes away. Closed statements which make it clear to her that you are not interested in what she has to say will—eventually—cause her to find someone who is more willing to listen to what she has to say.

> "I really don't know—and don't want to know—anything about that."
>
> "It's none of my business."
>
> "I don't feel comfortable talking about this."
>
> "That's not something I've ever been interested in."

3. Use your looming deadlines as a way to cut off or limit the chit-chat. In today's work environment, practically everyone has a deadline that is fast approaching—or has passed. Bowing out of a conversation with the explanation that you have a work issue that needs your attention is an acceptable, polite, and appropriate way to walk away from the chit-chat.

> "I really can't talk right now. I'm in the middle of a project I need to get done before the end of the day."
>
> "I'm really swamped right now. I can give you five minutes. But then I'm going to have to ask you to leave so I can get this project finished."

4. If you know Cathy is going to stop by, you can put an emergency plan into place. It's highly likely that if Cathy is bothersome to you, she also is to your co-workers. Form a type of support group where one of your co-workers comes to get you if you are still with Cathy after a set amount of time. Be careful with this, though. If Cathy finds out about it—directly or indirectly—you could be creating another problem.

Most of the time one of these techniques will lead to Cathy figuring out that you are not interested in chatting and she will look for someone else. However, some are so dedicated to chatting that they never catch on, even if you're direct and specific. In these situations, you will need to talk to your supervisor about the situation and get his or her assistance.

Mary Martyr

Yes, Joan of Arc is alive, well, and living in Mary Martyr's body. Lucky you, working for the same organization as Mary, providing you with the distinct honor of being able to observe—on a daily basis—what true dedication and loyalty are all about. Oh, that someday, you could be half the employee that she is!

Well, you get the picture. Sometimes you're not sure whether you feel guilty listening to her or whether you want to burn her at the stake. In most situations, Mary is simply looking for some appreciation and recognition that her work is valued. So give her what she needs. One-on-one is great, but you can get even better results out of giving her the feedback in front of her boss or her peers.

If you feel uncomfortable doing this verbally, write her an e-mail. Just make sure that you copy her boss on it!

> "I wish that some of the rest of us had the dedication that you show every day. Thanks a lot for your help."
>
> "I really appreciate the fact that I can depend on you to help out in a pinch. You always do it gladly and do a great job!"
>
> "Mary, thanks for putting in all the extra hours you did on ABC project. We all know it wouldn't have turned out as well as it did without you—and we wouldn't have gotten it done on time. On behalf of your teammates, Mary, thanks for all your hard work!"

Tommy the Thief

Tommy the Thief is not thinking about "borrowing" some of the company's pens or paper for use at home. He's a more dangerous thief—he's on the prowl to steal his co-workers' opinions, ideas, and suggestions that he can pass along to others—especially those in management—as his own. Tommy will also steal the credit for other people's hard work and thought.

He works very smoothly. In an innocent conversation you have with him, you mention an idea you have or voice your opinion. Most of the time, Tommy will act like he only half heard what you had to say. In reality, he's neatly filed away that information, waiting for the opportune time—which means before you've done anything with it—to pass on the idea, opinion, or suggestion as his own.

Tommy's victims are often flabbergasted when they hear their opinion or idea coming out of Tommy's mouth. They are amazed when the boss or others in management extol Tommy's brilliance. They are left speechless when their thoughts, ideas, and opinions end up in a touted report or memo authored by Tommy.

If you confront Tommy without concrete and undeniable evidence, you are most likely going to be met with denial. You will be tempted to argue that the two of you discussed the idea and Tommy ran with it before you did. In many situations, though, Tommy will likely deny ever having had the conversation with you, claiming to have been working on the idea, suggestion, or opinion for weeks (if not months). In the end, you will get nowhere, and simply end up more frustrated and angry than before you talked to him.

Realize that you are never going to win against Tommy unless you have documented proof of the theft. And you are not going to win points by going to your boss—or Tommy's boss—and trying to make a case for idea/suggestion/opinion theft. You are going to be the one who ends up looking like a sad and desperate character.

If the theft was of an idea that is going to be moved forward, think about whether it would be beneficial for you to relent on Tommy's denial of thievery and suggest that you work together on the project. You're not going to end up getting credit for the original idea, but at least you'll be involved in the planning and implementation. It might be wiser to make Tommy your ally than your enemy.

In the end, write this one off as a lesson learned the hard way. Be professional in your interactions with Tommy, but in the future limit your discussions with him to topics as innocuous as the weather, and the exact shade of blue he's wearing. Also, start taking personal actions that will minimize the possibility of this happening again, such as

- Put your ideas in writing immediately—even if you don't take action on them. Start an "ideas" folder on your computer and create a separate file for each of your ideas. Then, if something comes up, you have computer documentation of the time you first came up with the idea.

- E-mail your suggestions, ideas, and opinions to the appropriate person(s) with offers to discuss the subject face-to-face in more detail.

- Send your boss a weekly update on your activities, thoughts, and ruminations.

- Speak up at meetings.

- Make sure others are around when you present ideas, suggestions, and opinions.

If you feel like your boss is being a bit of a Tommy, see chapter 5 for tips on how to get the proper acknowledgment for your ideas and contributions.

Dealing with Other Difficult Personalities

If you didn't find a description of your difficult co-worker, don't despair. Here are some general guidelines that will help you deal more effectively with almost any challenging personality:

- **Watch nonverbals—both yours and the other person's.** When there ends up being a problem with a person, think about the nonverbals you saw when he or she was coming toward you. For example, the gossiper might have a habit of looking all around as he or she approaches to make sure that the "wrong" people aren't present; the person who is about to throw a temper tantrum often has balled fists. Many times, if you pay attention to people's body language, you are able to see a problem coming.

  Also, think about the message you may be sending with your body language. People often interpret body language literally and assume that if you are sitting with your arms and legs crossed, you are closed off, which might make them defensive and more "animated." It doesn't matter that you find this the most comfortable position to sit. Their perception (and therefore their reality) is that you are displaying negative body language.

- **Listen to understand.** People have a strong need to be listened to and understood. There are many people who will not let up on something until they get acknowledgement that they have been heard and understood. So put your concerns away and focus on understanding what that person is saying. If you're not familiar with active listening skills, spend some time reading up on them and then practice them—habitually.

  Once you think you understand what the person is saying, you need to check to make sure. You can use paraphrasing to verify that you understood the person's meaning, intent, criteria, issues, concerns, and so on. Some ways you can start the paraphrasing include the following:

  "Let me see if I've got this. You're concerned about _____ because _____. Is that right?"

  "So you think that _____, _____, and _____ are more important considerations on this project than _____ and _____?"

"Okay, if I understand what you're saying, _____.
Did I get it?"

- **Look for the positive.** This is not the easiest thing to do when all you can think of is getting away from the person. Start by realizing that, in the problem person's mind, his or her intention is good—and sometimes even righteous. Most employees are not purposefully pains-in-the-necks. They truly believe that they are being caring, conscientious co-workers. Believing that the basis of their action is good intentions will help you listen to them in a different way and, possibly, find the real issue.

- **Use "I/me/my" language.** That is, take responsibility for your feelings, impressions, and perspectives. When you own what you say, people are less likely to become defensive or have a negative reaction to what you are saying. It also makes it clear that what you are saying is your take on the situation and not the gospel truth. Use phrases such as

"Here's my take on this situation...."
"It may just be me, but I thought...."
"The way I see the situation is...."

- **Don't automatically assume that you've been wronged.** Sometimes you misunderstand or misread situations and a polite discussion can quickly clear things up. Start conversations with the assumption that you're seeking clarification rather than revenge.

"I think there might have been a mixup...."
"I'm not sure exactly what happened, but...."
"I think we might have misunderstood each other earlier...."

Regardless of the type of personality you are dealing with, it's important to recognize that both you and the other person are responsible for coming up with ways to work together effectively. You are both responsible for

- Dealing with each other politely
- Treating each other with respect
- Gathering information rather than jumping to conclusions
- Addressing the conflict before it gets out of hand
- Working together to find a mutually beneficial way of working effectively
- Recognizing that you are both part of the problem, as well as the solution
- Actively listening to the other person—seeking to understand the other person's perspective, views, and opinions rather than criticizing the person
- Not involving your co-workers in the situation (as in, "Well, let's go talk to Harry. He'll tell you the same thing I'm saying.")
- Trying to work out the situation yourselves before seeking input from management
- Acting with integrity

Conclusion: Not Everyone Is This Difficult to Work With

Every work environment is going to have difficult people. But don't let this override the fact that you will also work with some truly wonderful, helpful, kind people. Spend your efforts and energy on cultivating a good working relationship with these people and do your job to the best of your ability. Just realize that, from time to time, you are going to have to deal with some of these difficult characters. When that time comes, maintain a professional attitude and try some of the tips in this chapter.

CHAPTER 5 Developing a Positive Relationship with Your Boss

Whether you like it or not, your boss has a significant impact on your success. So, when things aren't going well, you need to look for ways to make the relationship more productive. And, if things are going smoothly with your boss, you need to nurture this critical association. Investing time in your relationship with your boss can result in greater job satisfaction and career growth. Unfortunately, individuals in their first jobs are focused on other more basic issues, such as learning the job, and can easily overlook this fact. Yet, it is important to recognize when a problem exists and then work to remedy the situation.

While attending a wedding ceremony several years ago, the guests were struck by the universal nature of the advice given to the new couple. The bride and groom were told that for any relationship to be successful, the effort that goes into the relationship from both people needs to equal 100 percent. For the workplace, this means that on days when your boss is giving 5 percent, you need to step up and give 95 percent. It doesn't matter that your boss is more experienced, and is supposed to set the example. What matters is that your boss's impact on your career is most likely greater than your impact on the boss. Keep this in mind as you think of ways to manage your relationship with the boss.

The Basics of Boss Relationships

Even if you have been in your job for a while, it's not too late to work on the basics. Reach out and get to know your boss better. Perhaps just finding out the answers to some of the following questions will start to turn the relationship in a more positive direction. Select the questions that are most relevant to your circumstance. Then, find opportunities to bring the questions forward informally, in your own words. I would suggest you do not ask all the questions at once. In addition to learning your boss's perspective, it might be helpful to informally tap into your co-workers' opinions on questions 2, 3, and 4. Learn the following:

1. What are your boss's goals? What is your boss trying to accomplish? How do you fit into the accomplishment of these goals?

2. What are the pressures your boss is under, and how might these pressures affect both you and your boss? What can you do in your job to help ease these pressures?

3. What is your boss's relationship with his or her boss? How does this relationship impact your work and career?

4. Why was your boss selected for the job? What specific skills and experiences does he or she bring that are needed for the organization's situation?

5. What does your boss expect of you, including daily work and long-term goals?

6. How does your boss prefer to receive information from you?

7. How does your boss prefer to give you ongoing feedback on your performance? How can you facilitate this feedback occurring?

How to Work with Challenging Bosses

Everyone has had at least one difficult boss at some point in his or her career. Perhaps your boss is unapproachable, or has so many direct reports that it is difficult for your results and needs to be noticed. Many times your boss's behavior has nothing to do with you and your work. It is important to first verify whether your boss's behavior is simply a reflection of his or her personality, approach, or pressing challenges, rather than his or her reaction to your performance. Then, determine the appropriate next steps to take.

You might be surprised that by learning more about your boss, your negative feelings might be turned into compassion for his or her situation.

If your relationship with your boss is not going well, no matter what, do not complain about your boss to other employees. If you need to vent, do so with friends outside of work. Comments made to other employees might be shared with your boss out of context, creating a worse situation. In addition, you could be labeled as a whiner, a label that can be difficult to overcome. Most people don't like working with or spending time with complainers. Most likely, your boss was selected for a business reason. So, focus on the positive and maximize your own performance. Also, think about what you can learn from the experience, and how that learning can help you now and in the future.

In the sections that follow, you will be given approaches to use with nine different types of bosses that can be problematic, including the boss who

- Is a poor performer
- Doesn't communicate
- Shows favoritism toward certain people
- Is hard to pin down for a meeting
- Takes credit for your work and ideas
- Is unapproachable
- Looks over your shoulder
- Has a large number of direct reports
- Pits direct reports against each other

Before you turn to the section that best describes your current boss, reflect on the following approaches that can apply to and help with all bosses, both good and bad:

- Give your boss constructive feedback in a positive way so that he or she clearly understands the impact the situation is having on you and your results.
- Keep track of your goals and accomplishments, and regularly update your boss and others impacted by your work.
- Establish a network within the company.

- From co-workers that you trust, seek to understand the reasons for the boss's behavior, by asking questions about their experiences. Make sure that you don't complain, but rather focus on listening for perspectives that might help you make adjustments during interactions with your boss.

- Be proactive in your approach to dealing with your boss, rather than being reactive or in a "wait-and-see" mode.

Your Boss Is a Poor Performer

From what you have observed, your boss isn't delivering the expectations that have been established because he or she lacks experience, skills, or desire. This situation is especially uncomfortable when bosses seem unaware of their shortcomings, or when their bosses criticize them in the presence of their employees. At a minimum, you aren't getting the coaching and direction you deserve and need. Also, the negative halo effect can shadow you, and diminish your impact and reputation. The negative halo effect occurs when a poor performer's direct reports are also viewed as ineffective. People who think that you also are ineffective will not be open to your ideas nor respect your opinions. When this happens, your future career potential might be limited.

To counter the negative effects of working for a poor performer, write short reports summarizing your accomplishments, and send them to your boss and other relevant individuals. Keep copies of the reports in a file, and consider keeping the file at home. Continue to believe in yourself and acknowledge your strengths.

Nicole Uses Her Strengths to Help Her Boss

In your situation, it might be that your strengths can counter the boss's shortcomings. This situation occurred for Nicole, so she decided to utilize her strengths with her boss, Jackie. Jackie was lacking in motivational communication skills. This was especially evident when Jackie shared department results and goals in staff meetings. Communication was one of Nicole's talents, so she offered to assist with that task, without being obvious about her reasons. By assisting her boss in this way, Nicole took some pressure off her boss so that Jackie could shift her focus to other responsibilities. Nicole's success with the department meetings reflected well on both her and Jackie.

Stay alert for open job positions within the organization. Doing so is especially important if you have been in your current job for some time. Make sure, though, that you are not getting into a potentially worse situation. And, before you get too serious about moving on, consider that a star performer could soon replace your boss.

Brad Predicts His Boss's Departure

You might be able to predict how soon your boss will be leaving based on the interactions between your boss and the hierarchy. This happened for Brad. He felt his boss Dan would be leaving shortly after a particularly difficult visit by the Marketing VP. Dan came into Brad's office after sharing his department's dismal results for the last quarter, extremely upset with how he had been treated by his boss and the VP. The pressure was building so greatly that Dan chose to leave before being fired.

If you haven't established a network in the company beyond your department, reach out to do so. Networking can help you learn much needed information about your department, and also gather perspectives about other bosses' strengths and weaknesses. One way to meet others is through company-sponsored activities, such as sports teams or volunteering opportunities. Even ride sharing has been a great source for network building.

Your Boss Doesn't Communicate

For whatever reason, your boss is not forthcoming in sharing the information that you need to do your job. These uncommunicative bosses sometimes view information as power, and believe that sharing information will somehow diminish their importance. Or, they just don't see it as worth the time it takes to share the data with all of their employees. They may even expect that their employees will learn what they need on their own, and will rarely follow up with direct reports to share relevant company news. Because of their heavy workload, some bosses just don't give a high priority to spending time on communicating with their employees. No matter what the reasons are, you might not be getting the information you need to complete your work properly, see how your work fits into the big picture, or further your career.

If you are at a point in a project where it is critical that you obtain information from your boss, set up a meeting. To ensure that you are well prepared, establish a clear purpose and agenda. Also have a list of questions you would like answered, and the reasons why knowing the information will help your results. A forthright approach is generally the most successful. If you are unable to set up a meeting with your boss in the office, attempt more informal approaches, such as connecting over lunch, or before group meetings start or after they end.

Keep your eyes and ears open for what you can learn from the informal network that was described in the preceding section. See what information your network has to fill in the blanks and answer your questions. Many organizations have regular newsletters or magazines. Make sure to read these publications carefully. If you have a question about an article and how it relates to your work, ask someone in your network, or send the question to your boss.

Kathy Adapts to a Long-Distance Boss

Kathy faced this communication gap after her company combined job positions in an effort to cut costs. One result was that her new boss was located in another state and in another time zone. Her previous boss had been located in the same office area as she was, so she saw him almost every day. Her new boss, Leonard, had people working for him across more than 10 states. Because of his heavy workload and travel schedule, Kathy saw him only once every two months and for no more than an hour. Kathy learned to utilize e-mail to communicate with Leonard. Also, Kathy spent more of her time talking directly to her customers to learn what they needed and expected, instead of trying to catch Leonard. She found that this was an effective approach to getting the information she needed.

Your Boss Shows Favoritism (and Not to You)

Throughout all aspects of life, people encounter the problem of favoritism. Individuals in positions of power are simply human, and can fail to maintain the discipline of consistency appropriate to their position. Whether it is parents, teachers, coaches, or bosses, there will be favorites. Inevitably, at some point in your career you will most likely be a "favorite." Sometimes just knowing that possibility exists can be helpful in dealing with this situation.

Some people who aren't the boss's favorite tend to try harder. Over time this situation can be demotivating if their awesome results don't change the behavior of the boss. These individuals can also become cynical if the "favorite" is not effective in his or her work, and is the favorite for reasons other than work performance. And finally, some individuals will jealously lash out at the "favorite." If they aren't careful, these reactions can lead to their own results suffering.

First, it is important to accept that some people will click together more than others due to common styles, backgrounds, or interests. Do not let your results drop because you aren't getting the positive reinforcement from your boss that you feel you deserve. Instead, share your successes and celebrate with family members or friends to get their acknowledgement. If you feel you aren't receiving the development you need, look for a mentor to give you career guidance and coaching. Identifying a mentor other than your boss is a good idea even when things are going well with your boss.

If you haven't already, ask your boss what he or she expects of you, and follow up with him or her on a regular basis seeking feedback. Instead of approaching your boss from a feeling of insignificance, approach him or her with confidence and interest in learning more about ways to improve your results further. Avoid sharing with your boss your concern about the treatment of the employee you perceive as the favorite. Your boss may interpret your concern as petty or inappropriate. Instead, focus on improving and maximizing your own results. If you have an ethical or legal concern, at some point it might make sense to seek advice from someone in the human resources department.

John Joins the Boss and His "Favorite" for Lunch

John had a success story because of his approach to a situation with his boss's "favorite." Soon after joining Mike's department, it was clear to John that Sam was Mike's favorite. Sam seemed to be in Mike's office whenever John stopped by for a planned meeting or an impromptu question. Mike and Sam went to lunch together in the cafeteria every day. John never saw anyone else sit with them over lunch.

Being relatively new with the company and brand new to Mike's area, John was not sure how to respond to this situation. Because Sam started with the company shortly before John did, they were able to relate well with each other. So, John asked Sam whether he could join him and Mike for lunch, and was told "of course." Once John joined them, others started to sit with them, which was a great way for John to expand his network. Although Sam was still clearly Mike's favorite, everyone felt better about being included in the lunchtime conversation.

Your Boss Is Hard to Pin Down for a Meeting

Why can't your boss just give you a few minutes of his or her time? Doesn't your boss see that this additional time will help the department's results? Some bosses project the impression that meeting with their employees is a waste of time. It is especially frustrating because you would expect bosses to be proactive about setting up meetings with their reports to review work status.

Unfortunately, the reality is that layers of management continue to be removed from organizational structures, resulting in bosses being given more responsibilities, more employees to manage, and yet no more time in the day. Many managers have reported that their workdays are 80 percent filled with meetings without enough critical alone time for other work they must accomplish. As a result, they are protective of this precious remaining time. Plus, some managers are so busy that they are either unable or unwilling to pick up cues from their employees that a significant issue requires their attention.

When you are in this situation with a boss who won't meet with you, it can lead to delayed decisions, which can cause you to miss deadlines. Or, you might move forward to meet the deadline without the boss's input and support. The risk is that down the road, he or she might express disapproval of what you have done, or may be blindsided by your actions. At that point, reminding your manager that you unsuccessfully tried to get his or her opinions will not help your situation.

Find out from your trusted peers whether your boss avoids everyone, or just you. Take comfort if your boss is this way with everyone who works for him or her, and keep trying to get the information you need. Instead of asking for a meeting, send a concise e-mail or voice-mail message, or find ways to stop in for quick, 5- to 10-minute discussions rather than lengthier meetings. See if your boss is available to discuss an issue over lunch or a cup of coffee. When you need an issue or problem resolved, succinctly state the issue, the options, and your recommendations.

If you have a question, help your boss understand how knowing the answer will assist in delivering what is required. For example, "Tom, which managers should I interview for input on the training content? I want to talk to people who are experienced and well respected by you and others, so that the training is well received." Regularly leave an e-mail or voice-mail message explaining the approach you plan to take, to keep your boss in the loop.

If you have learned that your boss is more open to meeting with your peers than with you, it's time for some honest self-reflection. Answer the following questions:

- Do you go to your boss with issues that might be viewed as trivial?
- Do you tend to use more time than perhaps is really needed?
- Do you come forward with problems and complaints, rather than staying upbeat and also offering solutions?

It might be that if you shift your approach slightly, your boss will be more open to sharing time with you. If other forms of communication won't work, and you need to request a meeting, provide the purpose succinctly and ask for a short time frame—even five minutes. Go in well prepared with a few key points on paper to share. Get comfortable leaving as soon as you have your needs met, rather than overstaying your welcome.

Your Boss Takes Credit for Your Work and Ideas

When your boss is taking credit for your accomplishments, others might not see your strengths and abilities, nor acknowledge your contributions. This action by your boss could have a negative effect on your career growth and development. You might be tempted to hold back your ideas from your boss. You must avoid this temptation because you risk negatively affecting your boss's perception of your creativity and productivity, and your results may suffer.

Judy and Her Boss Clash

Judy is excited about participating in a group presentation for the operations VP, who is in town for the day. The subject of the presentation is the novel approach she is taking to the rollout of the company's newest product. The VP is interested in learning about this approach, for possible application in other divisions. Judy has never met the VP, nor participated in a presentation of this magnitude. Her boss, Ken, is taking the lead, and Judy and three others in the room have small prearranged pieces of the presentation. Judy is stunned when Ken starts talking about her ideas and project as if they were his own. So, when it's her turn, she pointedly uses the words "I" and "my" repeatedly. Her boss seems miffed.

(continued)

(continued)

> When the presentation is over, Ken tells Judy that she is not a team player. Judy responds by asking Ken why he took credit for her work. Ken states back, "You just don't get it, do you? Since you work for me, I had a major role in the development of those ideas."

Consider that the responsibility for both successes and failures for the department rest with your boss. The head of the department is responsible to coach direct reports and help them achieve their portions of the department's goals. You often work in a team environment to accomplish your goals, so it can be difficult to differentiate your unique contributions from your boss's. In most cases, when the boss looks good, so do you. Knowing this information might be enough for you.

But if the above perspective does not alleviate your concerns, speak candidly with your boss about not being acknowledged for your talents and results. You might receive reassurance that your boss is aware of your contributions and is selling you to others in the organization during promotion and rating meetings. It is to the boss's advantage to have direct reports who are succeeding and doing well.

After speaking with your boss about your concern, you might still feel that your boss isn't selling you to others nor acknowledging your contributions. In fact, he or she might seem like a barrier to your creativity. In this case, make sure that you keep track of and regularly publish a summary of your goals and accomplishments. As previously mentioned, look for a mentor to provide career guidance and coaching.

Your Boss Is Unapproachable

Some bosses seem to be on the go constantly, and it's difficult to get their attention to talk about their weekend activities, or to even say hello. These bosses may be perceived as overly serious, aloof, gruff, or "all business." This situation might cause you to want to avoid as much contact as possible with your boss. Yet, avoiding contact with an unapproachable boss can hinder you from getting needed information and feedback, and can cause the work environment to become even more uncomfortable. Also, avoiding contact with your boss will negatively affect your career growth and advancement because the details of your accomplishments will be unknown.

Understanding the source of the behavior can help ensure that you stay communicative and continue to interact positively with your boss. There are multiple possible causes for your perception. Some bosses are extremely busy, both professionally and personally, and so are focused solely on maximizing the work they accomplish each day while at work. Or, if you have a light, extroverted style, and your boss is a more serious introvert, this contrast can cause the boss to appear unapproachable. Perhaps the boss's stress level is so high that he or she is not aware of the behavior's impact.

Glenda Proactively Approaches Her Unapproachable Boss

If you are confident in your relationship with your boss and comfortable giving feedback, use nonconfronting language to let him or her know what you notice and its impact on you. Glenda decided to take this action with her boss, Donna, who was the new human resources manager at a customer service center. Her background was in manufacturing work environments, where the pace was faster and the culture less relaxed than the customer service center. Also, Donna had a longer commute than in her previous job, yet did not want to sacrifice time with her family each day. So, Donna started her day at 7:00 a.m., while most of the office started at 8:00; she worked through lunch by eating at her desk, and left by 4:00 p.m. Donna was more businesslike in her interactions than what the human resources team was used to, so she came across to them as abrupt and unfriendly.

One morning Glenda came to Donna's office and asked whether she could speak to her for a few minutes. In a very matter-of-fact manner, Glenda said "Donna, I would like to get to know you better and have not been able to do so since you started. It seems that you are always in your office working or in a rush to go somewhere. Is there any way I can help this situation, and learn more about what is important to you?" Because of Glenda's tone and the words she used, Donna responded in a nondefensive manner. She explained her situation to Glenda, who then asked whether there was any work that she could take on to help with Donna's workload. Donna got back to her with some ideas, which helped Glenda in meeting her personal growth objectives and eased Donna's stress. Also, Donna adjusted her approach slightly so that the team members felt more comfortable with her.

If you are not confident about giving feedback as Glenda did, you can take another approach to address the situation. During a regular meeting with your boss, add to the agenda the desire to identify the common concerns and challenges that you share, and brainstorm possible approaches to addressing these common concerns. The brainstorming can provide an opening for offering help to address some of the challenges.

Your Boss Looks Over Your Shoulder

Working for a boss who is a micromanager is especially difficult if you have previously worked for a boss who gave you more of a free rein in setting goals and action plans to accomplish the goals. The boss who micromanages is checking up on you every step of the way. At times, you wonder whether these micromanagers have any work of their own because they seem to spend so much time questioning the work that you are trying to get done.

When your boss seems to always be looking over your shoulder, your creativity can be hindered because you are limited to your boss's way of thinking. Also, the focus on having to explain previous decisions and look to the past can reduce the amount of time and energy you have to spend on future planning. This management style can inhibit continual improvement in your areas of responsibility.

At the beginning of a new project, ask your boss what role he or she would like in the project. Schedule regular updates during the project's life, instead of waiting until the end of the project, or when your boss comes to you. This approach might be enough to allow your boss to back off some and give you the freedom you desire.

Your perception of micromanaging by the boss could be because he or she is more detail-oriented than you are. You might be more motivated by talking about and focusing on the big picture rather than the minutia. These types of bosses prefer to talk and think about the nitty-gritty facts. They might wrongfully conclude that you are not watching the details as closely as necessary because of your focus on the big picture. Be patient as you proactively communicate to help your boss gain confidence in your ability to manage the details. Or, if the boss is correct and you do need help with the details, ask for coaching and guidance to assist you in gaining this skill.

Some bosses tend to micromanage because they were "burned" in the recent past when they didn't closely monitor a project assigned to one of their employees. The employee's project failed due to the lack of abilities and experience, and the boss was held accountable and responsible for the failure. To ensure that their department isn't hurt again by an employee's poor performance, these bosses closely monitor work products. If this is the case with your boss, his or her confidence in you will increase over time, based on sustained, positive results. Take time to regularly communicate the barriers you encounter, and the ways you are addressing them. Be patient as you prove your abilities to your boss over time.

Your Boss Has Many Direct Reports

More and more people find themselves sharing their bosses with countless others. With levels of middle management being cut, the remaining managers have more responsibility in addition to having to manage and coach additional employees. If you and your boss are in this situation, it might be difficult to develop a meaningful work relationship. If your boss is not aware of your contributions, skills, and future career desires, you might not get the future assignments that you desire.

Actively work to develop your boss's trust in you, without being a time drain. Trust is developed over time, with positive experiences and impressions. Ask your boss the communication method he or she prefers. If the preference is e-mail, provide a detailed subject heading, and do not overuse the e-mail signal requesting an urgent response. It is common for managers to receive more than 100 incoming e-mails each day. So, if e-mail is the method your boss prefers, find out what you can do to ensure that your message is one that is read and responded to in a timely manner. Whether the preference is e-mail, phone calls, or in-person communication, respect your boss's limited time and ensure that you are concise and clear about what you share and any needs you have.

Identify ways to stand out from the crowd of subordinates. Tell your boss what is going well for you, the challenges you are experiencing, and the ways you are addressing the challenges.

Ramona Takes Some of the Load Off Her Boss

Creatively determine what you might do to help alleviate your boss's workload. Ramona, the company's receptionist, was able to do this successfully with Dean, her boss. Dean was newly promoted to his position, which was a combination of the responsibilities of two previous managers. While learning his job responsibilities and getting to know the 25 people who reported directly to him, Dean was told that he also needed to become certified as a Management Trainer in time management, and train two classes each month. As a trainer, he was expected to manage the room logistics, supplies, and ordering of the food for the trainees, in addition to becoming a subject-matter expert.

While Dean was working long hours, Ramona was bored, without enough to do. During one especially harried day for Dean, Ramona offered to help with the training, suggesting she could order the food. In a short time, Ramona was also handling the room logistics and supplies for Dean *and* all the other trainers. This expanded role made for quicker and more interesting days, and resulted in Ramona becoming an administrative assistant, a role that she wanted.

Another way to stand out is to look for business news articles of relevance to your boss's work and forward these articles, with a short note. As you select what you are going to send, keep in mind the already heavy workload and incoming mail. The note you add can help your boss glean key points and determine what best to do with the article.

Your Boss Pits Direct Reports Against Each Other

Many bosses meet regularly with their team. This meeting is an opportunity for the boss to productively share information and for team members to share updates on what is happening in their areas. This approach makes sense, and seems like a sound management technique. Unfortunately, many bosses turn this meeting into a competitive match, pitting team members against each other. As team members report their results, the boss makes comments like "Jerry, your production efficiencies are significantly below the others here. Just look at what Carla has done to motivate her team." Many times these types of comments are made in a joking way, yet they can still fracture a collaborative team spirit.

This approach doesn't serve any purpose other than to cause team members to feel uncomfortable and inappropriately competitive with each other. Instead of motivating people to work together for a common goal or purpose, the boss's creation of this destructive internal competition can lead to poorer overall results, a reduction in sharing of information, less cooperation, and an internal rather than external focus.

Responding to this type of boss is difficult because it requires addressing a negative culture that the boss has created and is sustaining. If you have positive relationships with other team members, talk privately and candidly with them about your concerns. Express your desire to work collaboratively rather than competitively. If enough of you share this desire, you have two options:

1. Continue to work together, ignoring the boss's attempts to pit you against each other, or

2. Go to the boss jointly and share your concerns and wishes. Your choice of options depends on your standing in the company and your relationship with your boss. If you decide to speak directly with your boss, share the positive impact on the organization's results that you would expect from a more collaborative culture.

If you are not able to find or influence others who want a more collaborative culture, you will need to decide whether you can survive your boss's regime and stay, or leave to find a culture that fits better with your preferences. Before proceeding, give this decision much thought and seek the counsel of others.

If Your Relationship with Your Boss Is Great

If your relationship with your boss is going along okay now, take advantage of the opportunity presented to you. For your professional development and career growth, look for ways to expand your role and impact. Also, use your creativity by trying new approaches and ideas in your current job. Notice the traits your boss exhibits that cause you to view him or her in a positive way. Determine which of those traits will come most naturally for you as you move into a position where you will be managing others. Go out of your way to get coaching from your boss to further your professional development.

Conclusion: Key Points to Remember About Developing a Positive Relationship with Your Boss

At some point in your career, you will most likely be a boss, and most likely you will want to be considered one of the favorite bosses rather than one of the most dreaded ones. So, on those days when you are working hard to make up for your boss's deficiencies, keep in mind that what you are learning now will help you to be a more effective boss in the future. Remember the following tips when you encounter tough situations with your boss.

What to Do if Your Boss Is a Poor Performer

- Write short reports summarizing your accomplishments and send them to your boss and other relevant team members.
- Find ways to use your talents to offset your boss's weaknesses.
- Stay alert for open job positions within the organization.
- Establish or strengthen a network to help you stay in the flow of communication.

What to Do if Your Boss Doesn't Communicate

- Meet with your boss and have a list of questions you would like answered, with the reasons why the information will help your results.
- Keep your eyes and ears open to learn needed knowledge from the informal network.
- Try using e-mail and assess how your boss responds.
- Talk directly to the recipients of your work to learn what they need.

What to Do if Your Boss Shows Favoritism

- Accept that some people will click together more than others.
- Look for a mentor to give you career guidance and coaching.
- Ask your boss what he or she expects of you, and regularly seek feedback.

- Focus on improving and maximizing your own results, rather than concerning yourself with the favorite employee.

What to Do if Your Boss Is Hard to Pin Down for a Meeting

- Send a short e-mail or voice-mail message when you need an issue resolved or a question answered.
- See whether your boss is available over lunch or a cup of coffee.
- If you have a problem or issue, come forward with various solutions or options and your recommendations.
- Request short meetings, send your agenda ahead of time, and come well prepared.

What to Do if Your Boss Takes Credit for Your Work and Ideas

- Acknowledge your boss's contributions to your success.
- Share your concerns with your boss about others' awareness of your results.
- Keep track of and publish a summary of your goals and accomplishments.
- Actively look for a career mentor to provide guidance and coaching.

What to Do if Your Boss Is Unapproachable

- To increase your understanding of the situation, identify the possible cause(s) for this behavior.
- Stay communicative and interact positively with your boss.
- Use nonconfronting language to let him or her know what you notice and its impact on you.
- During a meeting with your boss, identify common concerns and challenges, share your perspectives, and offer assistance.

What to Do if Your Boss Looks Over Your Shoulder

- At the beginning of a project, ask your boss what he or she would like his or her role to be in the project.

- Instead of waiting until the end of the project, or when your boss comes to you, schedule regular project updates.

- Proactively communicate to help instill confidence in your ability to manage the details.

- Regularly communicate barriers and the ways you are addressing them, to help prove your abilities.

What to Do if Your Boss Has a Large Number of Direct Reports

- Ask your boss his or her preferred method of communication. Be concise and clear in what you share.

- Tell your boss what is going well, and the ways you are addressing your challenges.

- Identify ways to stand out from the crowd of subordinates— look to expand your role in a way that can help reduce your boss's workload, or forward articles of relevance with a short note.

What to Do if Your Boss Pits Direct Reports Against Each Other

- Share your concerns with trusted peers, and decide to work together collaboratively, despite your boss's behavior.

- Go to your boss and share your concerns with the culture that has been created, what you would suggest, and the reasons it would be an improvement for the organization's results.

- If you stand alone in a desire to change the culture, determine whether you are willing and able to stay and endure your boss's regime.

CHAPTER 6

Eight Ways to Be an Effective Team Member

You're probably thinking, "Oh, come on. I know how to be a team player. I went to college on a sports scholarship, I worked on the college newspaper, and I worked on team projects in half of my classes. I know about a being a team player!" However, what it took to be a good team player in those situations might not be the same skills that are required to be a successful, effective, *work* team member.

Being an effective team player is not simple—it takes skill, practice, and effort. Many times people fail to put in the time and effort required to be a good team member because they get so caught up in the job that individual survival overrides the concern for and focus on the team. This could end up being your undoing because the ability to be an effective team member is one of the most highly valued attributes an employee can bring to a job.

One of the best ways to become a better team member is to develop an understanding of some of the characteristics an effective team member displays. Once you develop that understanding, you can begin to take conscious actions to incorporate those characteristics into your day-to-day behavior. This chapter is designed to help you start on the journey to being an effective team member by looking at eight characteristics that effective team members demonstrate.

1. Hone Your Oral Communication Skills

Most people who have mastered the English language (or think they have) consider themselves to be good communicators. However, an ability to speak a language properly and clearly does not necessarily make a person an effective communicator. To be effective, you need to be understood by the people to whom you are speaking (and you need to understand them). If that doesn't happen, true communication has not occurred—regardless of how eloquent your verbal delivery happens to be.

Check for Understanding

Sometimes you're not going to feel confident that what you have said has been understood completely or properly. When it's a critical communication, and it's vital that the person understand you properly, you might want to check for understanding. For example, you might say "I want to make sure I said what I really meant to say. What was your understanding of what I just said?"

Or you can try a self-deprecating approach (if that fits your style) with something like, "I think I may even have confused myself on that. What did you get out of what I just said?" Questions such as this will help you verify that what you thought you said to the other person is what the other person actually heard. If there is a disconnect, you will have the opportunity to clear up the misunderstanding before it becomes a problem.

Before you go any further, do the following exercise.

Communication Exercise
There are three parts to communication: words, tone of voice, and nonverbals (for example, gestures and facial expressions). In the following chart, indicate what percentage of a message you think a person receives through each of these three parts (for a total of 100 percent of the message):

Words	_____% of the message
Tone of voice	_____% of the message
Nonverbals	_____% of the message
	100% of the message

If you are like most people, you gave a relatively high percentage to "words" and a relatively low percentage to "nonverbals." It might surprise you to find out that the vast majority of communication has less to do with what you say and more to do with how you say it. Words, in fact, make up only about 7 percent of the message, with tone of voice being about 38 percent and nonverbals being about 55 percent of the message.

Of course, every lesson must come with a disclaimer. Although these numbers came from solid research on the part of Dr. Albert Mehrabian, you can't use these statistics to guide every communication scenario. For example, the breakdown doesn't work effectively in written communication—such as e-mail—or during telephone conversations. Regardless, the point to remember is that in face-to-face communication, there is a significant part of your message that comes from components other than your words.

Enhancing Face-to-Face Communication

There are three ways you can enhance the effectiveness of face-to-face communication:

1. **Recognize that your nonverbal communication speaks louder than your words.** It is impossible for you not to communicate nonverbally. Even if you sit motionless, staring unblinkingly at a wall, you are communicating. (Try it. I guarantee someone will come up and try to figure out what you're staring at and then ask you what you're doing.) If you're not sure whether your nonverbal communication is positive and open, ask someone you trust how you could improve your nonverbal communication.

2. **Communicate earlier rather than later.** Sometimes you might see or hear someone doing or saying something that makes you angry. Instead of dealing with it, you let it fester. In the end, this kind of behavior may result in you trying to avoid that person and, as a result, isolating you from your team or that person. If you have a problem with someone on your team, talk to the person about it as soon as possible using effective conflict-management skills (see chapter 7). You will either end up solving the problem or find out that your interpretation was off base. Either way, you've shown that you are willing to work out problems with your team members rather than display inappropriate and ineffective behaviors.

3. **Provide positive feedback.** All of us enjoy working with people who recognize our talents and contributions. To paraphrase Confucius, "The effective team member helps others to realize what is good in them; he does not help them to realize what is bad in them. The small team member does the opposite." Look for opportunities to legitimately pump up your fellow team members, but remember these guidelines:

- Follow the four feedback "musts": be specific, make it job related, be timely, and don't make it painful for the recipient. (See page 123 for more information on the four "musts.")

- Think about the reaction from the receiver. Not everyone is going to be visibly thrilled to receive public feedback, for example. "Receiving Feedback" on page 127 will help you better deal with and understand the different reactions you might receive.

- Keep in mind your organization's culture when giving feedback.

- Remember that size does *not* matter when it comes to giving positive feedback. Recognize the little contributions that your fellow team members make that help move something forward, make something a little easier, are helpful, and so on, as well as the major contributions.

- Be sincere. Don't stretch to find positive feedback for someone, or try to turn something the receiver of the feedback knows was not good into a positive. If the feedback is not genuine, sincere, and perceived by the person receiving the feedback as something worthy, you are going to be viewed negatively, suspiciously, or, potentially, as having ulterior motives.

If you need to improve your oral communication skills, you might also want to check the communication information in chapter 1.

2. Improve Your Listening Skills

While listening is often combined with communication, it is a skill that is significant enough—and severely under-utilized enough—to merit its own category.

First, you must distinguish between hearing and listening. Hearing is a physical ability to transmit sound waves to the brain. Listening is a conscious choice a person makes to focus on another person. Active listening is a choice a person makes to mentally and physically attend to what another person is saying.

How to Be a Good Listener

Good listeners are critical to the effective functioning of a team. That means that every team member needs to

- Choose to absorb, understand, consider, and discuss ideas and viewpoints with others.

- Be interested in learning from others as well as sharing his or her knowledge and skills.

- Be willing to admit that he or she might not always have the right answer or the only answer to what the team is facing.

- Be willing to listen first and speak second—or not at all.

Characteristics of Active Listeners

Think about people you've talked to whom you felt truly listened to you and cared about what you had to say. Chances are, they demonstrated some of the following behaviors of active listeners:

- Look at the person who is speaking to you—not at the wall, out the window, at anyone else, or anywhere else. When you look at the person, you send the message that you are interested in what he or she has to say.

- Ask probing questions. To say that you have listened effectively and actively requires that you have understood, as fully as possible, what the person is trying to tell you. That often requires you to ask probing questions (see the following box) to develop that understanding.

Probing Questions
■ "Tell me more about _____"
■ "Would you be more specific about _____?"
■ "Could you give me an example of _____?"

- Ask others' opinions before you present your opinion. Too often people are more interested in swaying another person to their way of thinking—right or wrong—than they are in learning something new. Take a chance to learn something new or see something in a different light by asking others for their ideas instead of shouting out your ideas first. You will also gain the respect of others when you listen to their ideas.

- When you are listening, just listen. Don't plan a response to something the speaker has said. Don't get ready to argue. Don't judge what the speaker is saying. Don't fiddle, fidget, or play with things on your desk. Don't do anything but listen to understand. If there is something that you feel that you are going to need to respond to and don't want to lose the thought, jot it down and then go back to focusing on understanding what the other person is saying.

- Paraphrase to check for understanding. What we think we heard and understood is not always what the other person wanted to say or actually said. When there is the slightest doubt in your mind that you and the other person are on the same wavelength, use paraphrasing to check for understanding. If your understanding is on target, the person will say so—and will appreciate you checking. If you're off base, the person will take the time to clarify what he or she was saying. Either way, you win by understanding what the person wanted to communicate.

- Listen for areas that you agree with what the person is saying rather than areas of disagreement. Too often, we focus on the words or phrases that we dislike and fail to realize that we see eye-to-eye on most things. If we listen for commonality, we minimize differences, making it easier to reach agreement and move on.

- Give the speaker encouragement. A nod, smile, eye contact, and other encouraging nonverbal gestures as well as verbal encouragement ("yes," "I see," or "OK" for example) shows the person that you are listening to understand.

3. Follow the Commit—Act—Results Formula

We are all human (although you might doubt that about some people, believe me, they are still human). As a result, we are flawed—we make mistakes. With that said, there is still nothing more irritating than working with someone who does not take responsibility for contributing, fails to take action or follow through on his or her commitments, or refuses to accept accountability for his or her results (or lack thereof). The Commit—Act—Results formula will help you avoid these barriers to good teamwork.

Commit

At the beginning of an assignment, task, or project, you should verbally commit to the action that you are going to take. When you say, "I will be responsible for doing X,"—and mean it—you are demonstrating a willingness to be a team player and accept responsibility for something that needs to be done. It also means that you are taking the responsibility to ensure that you completely understand what you are supposed to do. That generally involves clarifying a number of things:

- What you are supposed to do
- Who else you will be working with or need to include (if anyone)
- Why it is important
- What the results need to look like
- When you need to have it done
- What resources you will have—or will need—to accomplish it

In many situations, it is helpful if you put your understanding of these things in writing. Then provide a copy of the document to the other person and review it with him or her for completeness and accuracy. There are three benefits of doing this:

- If there is any misunderstanding, it can be cleared up immediately, enhancing the likelihood of your success.
- It serves as a checklist or reference point while you are working on the task, project, or assignment to make sure you are on track and on time.
- At the end of the task, project, or assignment, you can use it to make sure that you have followed through and completed everything to which you agreed.

When you accept responsibility, it means that you are going to do what you agreed to do, knowing that you—and only you—are accountable for your results—or lack of results.

Act

If you said you were going to do something within a designated time-frame, do it. No excuses. No whining.

Mark Lets a Roadblock Stop Him from Following Through

To prepare for an upcoming customer audit, Jennie needed some data off a computer program she didn't know how to operate. Mark, another person on the team, had access to the program and was fairly competent on it. Jennie told Mark what she needed and when she needed to receive it. Mark agreed to get the data to her when she needed it.

The day it was due, Jennie dropped in on Mark to find out exactly what time he would be able to get the data to her and was met by a blank stare from Mark. It seems that there were three levels of access on the program and he only had Level 1. Accessing the data Jennie needed required Level 2 access. Mark had called IT and left a message requesting Level 2 access. His call was never returned and he promptly forgot about his commitment to Jennie.

Mark's response was, "Well, I would have gotten it to you, but IT never returned my call for an access upgrade. I guess I just forgot about it."

Mark's response doesn't cut it. There are simply no acceptable reasons—no allowable excuses—for not following through on your commitments.

Yes, obstacles and roadblocks do occur and other priorities come up. When that happens—and you absolutely cannot get around, over, through, or under the complication—you need to go back to the person, team, or team leader and get assistance or renegotiate your timeframe on the assignment.

Mark and Jennie Work Together to Find a Solution

"Do you have any idea how critical this data is to the audit? Yeah, ABC Company is one of our smaller customers right now, but if this audit goes well, there is the potential for them to do four to five times as much business with us starting next year," Jennie said.

"Nobody told me that!," Mark said.

"I shouldn't have to tell you! Well, I guess I should have. But either way, you made a commitment. Now I'm stuck. Isn't there some way this can get done before 3 p.m. today?" responded Jennie.

Luckily Mark rose to the occasion and they were able to come up with a plan of attack—with Jennie helping out on a few things. She got the data that she needed to get her part of the report done on time and no one else on the team was any the wiser. Mark, however, learned a valuable lesson on following through on his commitments. This situation had a happy ending. Unfortunately, too many don't.

When you fail to follow through, you let your team members down—and you let the whole team down. Pretty soon, your co-workers will stop believing in you, stop trusting you, and start seeing you as unreliable. To avoid this:

- Keep a record of your commitments someplace where you will constantly be reminded of them.

- If you run into a roadblock, ask your teammates or team leader for help.

- Put the deadlines for commitments on your calendar—every calendar you have (such as computer, wall, and cell). Don't rely on someone else to remind you when you're supposed to be somewhere, what you're supposed to do, or what you're supposed to bring.

- Avoid procrastinating. You never know what kinds of problems you can run into. It's always better to get things done in a quality manner a little earlier than to produce a mediocre or poor-quality product just in the nick of time.

Results

If you've followed through on your commitment to be responsible for something, then you've already addressed the results part. Results is the outcome—the end of the task, project, or assignment. It's important to recognize that whether you like it or not, you are accountable for your results, which come from the decisions and actions you take within the work environment. Results is about being willing to be held accountable for your efforts—good or bad. You are accountable, as a team member as well as an individual contributor, for

- What you do

- When you do it

- How you do it

- Why you did what you did
- How well you did it

The key is to own up to your own actions or inaction. Don't make excuses. Don't blame others. The only one who can be held account-able for you not being a responsible adult is you! You will—believe it or not—actually win points by stepping up to the plate and accept-ing responsibility for errors or omissions that are your fault. The critical step, then, is to do something about it. For example, "That was my fault. I said I would do it and it completely slipped my mind. I apologize to everyone. I'll work late tonight and have it for every-one first thing in the morning. Will that be OK?"

So, in the event that you let your boss or team down, you are also accountable for

- Owning up to the mistake
- Coming up with a plan to fix the situation
- Fixing the situation
- Learning from the situation
- Not making the same mistake again

4. Learn How to Give and Receive Feedback Effectively

As a member of a team, you will often be in a position to give feed-back to your co-workers as well as receive it from them. This section will help you handle both sides of the feedback equation more effec-tively. Let's start with the easy stuff: giving positive feedback.

Giving Positive Feedback

Positive feedback is not just something that your boss or team leader should be giving to employees. Anyone can give positive feedback to anyone else in the organization who has done something good, pos-itive, or helpful.

I haven't met a single person who hasn't appreciated receiving posi-tive feedback. Some are shy about receiving it; some are embar-rassed; some are jubilant; some are downright shocked. But they all appreciate you noticing their effort or good work.

> ## Kurt Makes Ingrid's Day with Positive Feedback
>
> On a referral, Kurt, a consultant, called Mega-Bits Company to set up an appointment. The receptionist, Ingrid, was one of the most pleasant and efficient front-desk people Kurt had dealt with in months. Kurt made an appointment with the company's president, Juan, for a meeting the following week. When Kurt showed up for the meeting, Ingrid was just as impressive in person as over the phone. As Kurt was leaving, he stopped at the front desk and gave Ingrid positive feedback. With every word Kurt said, Ingrid's smile got wider and her eyes got brighter.
>
> Kurt didn't have another appointment at the company for over a week. But when he opened the front door, Ingrid's face lit up and she welcomed Kurt by name. Not only did he reinforce her for doing good work, he made his working relationship with her—and the company—even better.

The Four "Musts" of Positive Feedback

There are four "musts" when giving positive feedback to ensure that the recipient will appreciate and value it.

The Feedback Must Be Specific

One of the reasons for giving anyone feedback is to encourage them to repeat the behavior. The only way they can do that is if they know specifically what they did that is being recognized.

Read through these two examples of feedback. If you were Ben, which one would you prefer to receive and why?

1. "Hey, Ben, thanks for the help on that report. I don't think I could have finished it without your help. You've got some talent!"

2. "Hey, Ben, thanks for the help on the Q1 Budget Variance Report. I don't think I could have finished it without your help. You've got a real talent for developing clear, understandable color charts and graphs. Everyone was really impressed. I made sure they knew that you did them. Thanks!"

Most people would prefer to receive the feedback in the second example because it tells you two things:

- Exactly what you did that was good/right/exceptional
- What good/right/exceptional looks like

Make Sure the Feedback Is Job-Related

Any feedback you provide to another person in a work environment needs to relate to some aspect of work, not something personal. The whole idea behind the positive feedback is to reinforce constructive *work* behaviors—behaviors that help you, the team, and the company.

Exercise: Feedback

Read through the following examples and mark the ones—if any—that you do *not* feel are appropriate.

❑ "The way you've modified the XB-100 machine has really helped get the production level up. We're going to exceed everyone's expectations now. Thanks!"

❑ "You've really changed your wardrobe over the last few weeks. Now you're looking young, sexy, and vital instead of like some dowdy old spinster. I like the look. Keep it up!"

❑ "I sure appreciate your sense of humor in these team meetings. Sometimes they get so serious that I think we stop focusing on what we need to be doing."

❑ "Thanks for jumping in there and saving the meeting this morning. I don't know where you come up with these creative ideas, but it was just what we needed to get unstuck. Thanks!"

Hopefully you recognized that the only one that doesn't belong in that list is the second one because it violates the second must: The feedback must be job-related. Not only that, it is in violation to most companies' anti-harassment policies. And it might set up the speaker and his employer for a sexual harassment lawsuit!

It Must Be Given in a Timely Manner

"Timely" means providing feedback as soon as humanly possible after the event occurred. The logic is that the closer in time the event and feedback occur, the more perceived value the positive feedback has and the more genuine it is perceived to be. Positive feedback looses credibility—as do you—the longer it is between the event and the positive feedback.

Don't Punish the Recipient

Here's another quick test for you. Put a checkmark in the box next to the example(s) of acceptable feedback.

- ❑ "Joe, you did a great job on Project Alpha. It really helped us get the new business from them. I never would have expected that kind of work out of you. The world is full of good surprises! Thanks!"

- ❑ "Eva, you're not half the idiot I thought you were (ha! ha!) Just kidding. Hey, you did a great job retooling that old piece of junk I have to operate in production room 2. I don't think it's run that well in 10 years!"

- ❑ "Harry, I just saw our team's production report for last month. I see that you were able—every day—to keep your production 10–15 percent above target. That's pretty impressive—for you. Keep it up!"

- ❑ "I'm hearing great things about the presentation you did during the Process Improvement Team meeting this morning on new product development. You really made our department look good with all the hard work you put into that. The main reason I stopped by, though, is to ask you about this mess of charts you gave me for the monthly review. I don't know how you expect me to make sense out of this mess. I need something I can work with; and if I don't get it, I'm not going to be happy."

- ❑ "Salvador, I just looked at the proposal you put together for the Attaboc Company. That is exactly what I was looking for—and more. You thought of things that even I didn't! I wish I could be as positive about the data analysis you did for Xycolam Company, though. I thought it was shallow and, in some instances, misleading. Your Attaboc Company proposal, though, was absolutely top-notch. Thanks!"

Unfortunately, not a single one of these examples is acceptable feedback. Every one of them is negative or derogatory in some way. Feedback becomes punishing when there is some kind of "pain" associated with it. In the first example, most people are going to find it painful to hear another person express amazement at their ability to do well. The third example is similar in terms of delivering pain after you have built the person up.

In the second example, the recipient is called an idiot, but the assumption is that, since it is delivered in a humorous manner, it's not an insult. Wrong! Whenever you say something derogatory to an individual—whether seriously or in a misguided attempt at humor—it is absolutely, positively, unequivocally unacceptable.

In some situations, you are going to have both positive feedback and constructive feedback to pass on to a person, as in the fourth example. The temptation is to get everything taken care of at once. Nothing could be less constructive. When you give positive feedback followed by constructive feedback (or, in this case, outright criticism without anything constructive to it), you will lose all of the value of the positive feedback because all the person will remember is the criticism. And, no, it does not make any difference if you put the constructive feedback first and follow it with the positive feedback.

When you have constructive feedback and positive feedback to give to a person, they should be shared at separate times. There is no hard-and-fast rule about which you should provide first. One way of deciding is to ask yourself, "Which of these is more important?" The answer should tell you which to talk to the person about now, and which to put off until a little later.

The final example is called a "sandwich"—a piece of good news, followed by a piece of bad news, topped off with another piece of good news. As with the previous example, it is guaranteed that the good news will get lost and the only thing the other person will "hear" and remember is the bad news. Again, provide both pieces of feedback, just at separate times.

Good Examples of Feedback

Now that you know what feedback should *not* look like, it's only fair that you get a few examples of what it *should* look like:

- "Eva, I can't begin to thank you for the help you gave me on the QA report this morning. There is no way I would have been able to get from where I was to the final product without your help. And, I got it to my boss on time. Thanks!"

- "José! I didn't have a chance to get to you this morning. Thanks for pulling that data off Pro-Tech for me. I have a feeling that, since I didn't ask you until late yesterday for help, you stayed late last night and ran it for me or came in early today. Having it on my desk this morning gave me some extra time to make sure the report was the best I could do. I stuck a note on the report so Martin [the boss] knows that it looks as good as it does only because of your help. Thanks!"

- "I got your notes from yesterday afternoon's Project Delta meeting. You really took good, detailed, understandable notes. Matter of fact, your notes are better than the notes I take when I'm there. I really appreciate you covering for me. I owe you one! Thanks."

Receiving Feedback

As important as it is to know how to give effective positive feedback, you need to understand the receiving end of positive feedback. In general, people tend to respond to positive feedback in one of four ways.

1. **The happy recipient.** These people visibly enjoy receiving feedback. Many of them start grinning from ear to ear. People who thoroughly enjoy getting positive feedback make it a true joy to give it. While they may not all respond with great enthusiasm, just their joyful "thank you" or "I appreciate it!" tells all. Any way you look at it, these are the ones who make it immediately rewarding to give positive feedback.

Ella Enjoys Positive Feedback

Ella is the administrative assistant to the COO. In many situations, administrative assistants fade into the woodwork as long as they're doing their job. There was nothing fading about Ella. To say she personified high-quality, responsive customer service was to sell her short.

After a couple of interactions with her, Tori, a new operations manager, took the time to give her very specific, genuine positive feedback. When Tori finished, Eva threw her hands in the air, waved them with sports-fan enthusiasm, said, "Touchdown!" and did a little victory dance.

---

2. **The embarrassed recipient.** When some people receive positive feedback, they turn red, study their feet, twist their hands, and do just about everything else they can to shy away from the attention. You get the impression that they are uncomfortable getting feedback—and they are. Quite often these people are not used to receiving positive feedback and they don't know how to graciously accept it. So, they twist and turn and mumble something that you think sounds like "thank you" before they turn and almost run away. Other people are embarrassed about receiving positive feedback due to cultural norms.

In either case, the temptation is to say that since it is so uncomfortable for that person to receive feedback, you will simply stop. You rationalize that then the person doesn't have to go through that painful experience. Do not, under any circumstance, stop giving these people positive feedback. Do, though, look at how and where you are giving it. If you're doing it in front of other people, for example, consider giving them feedback in a more private place. Be patient with these people. It is going to take a while for them to feel comfortable with the positive reinforcement, to believe that you truly do appreciate what they did, and to believe that you are, in no way, trying to embarrass them.

3. **The suspicious recipient.** This person has been a victim of the "positive feedback followed by a kick in the behind" approach so often that they are gun shy. To them, getting positive reinforcement only means one thing—they are going to be in trouble for something else. As soon as you start the positive reinforcement, these people are waiting for the "but" to come in (as in "You did a great job on X, BUT, why can't you ever manage to get Y done on time?").

Initially, you will probably not get much of a response from these individuals. After you have walked away a few times without giving them the "but," they will start to soften up. Eventually, they will realize that your positive reinforcement is genuine and straightforward. Then, they will start to thaw and you'll begin getting "thank you" responses.

4. **The dismissive recipient.** The fourth response you might encounter in giving positive feedback is the person who says something like, "Oh, it was nothing" or "I was just doing my job." When you receive this kind of response to your positive feedback, the temptation is to stop giving this person feedback because they don't really appreciate it. Nothing could be further from the truth. It is just difficult for some people to verbally accept positive reinforcement. It doesn't mean that inside they are not jumping up and down with joy. So, even if you don't get the kind of response you think you should—or you would like to get—in response to your positive feedback, don't stop giving it.

Giving Constructive Feedback

Now we need to move on to the more difficult feedback skill: giving constructive feedback. But get the idea of "criticism" out of your mind. Criticism is negative, hurtful, and does not help a person improve.

Constructive feedback is a face-to-face conversation with another person where you share your personal observation of a problem behavior in a way that will help the individual grow and develop and that will contribute to building a relationship built on honesty and genuine concern for the other person.

Let's break down that rhetoric and address this issue with a short quiz.

Exercise: Feedback		
For each statement, mark whether it is True (T) or False (F). You'll find the answers at the end of the chapter.		
	True	**False**
1. To make constructive feedback meaningful, start it with phrases such as "you said…," or "you did…."	_____	_____
2. "You are always rude during the Project Brainee Team meetings, like when you said _____ today," is acceptable constructive feedback.	_____	_____
3. The only thing that matters in giving constructive feedback is the present. It doesn't matter that the person has demonstrated this same behavior in the past.	_____	_____
4. When giving constructive feedback, you should provide the person with all the relevant information at your disposal regarding his or her behavior.	_____	_____
5. Constructive feedback should focus on what the person is doing rather than who the person is.	_____	_____

(continued)

(continued)

	True	False
6. "Everyone hates it when you and Nicole argue during team meetings, like when you started arguing about ____ this morning." is acceptable constructive feedback.	____	____
7. Feedback should be given to help, not to hurt.	____	____
8. A good general rule of thumb to follow is that constructive feedback should be given within 48 hours of the person's behavior.	____	____
9. When giving someone constructive feedback, you should also give them advice on improving.	____	____

There are a variety of approaches for giving constructive feedback. One of the easiest to remember is

I feel [emotion] when you [person's behavior] because [impact of person's behavior].

For example:

I feel frustrated when you take actions without discussing them with the rest of the team because it makes me feel like my opinions and preferences aren't important.

I was distracted when you and Jane were joking around during the meeting because I couldn't hear what other people were saying.

Receiving Constructive Feedback

The other issue that is important with constructive feedback is learning how to listen to and appreciate receiving constructive feedback. Listening to constructive feedback—whether it's solicited or unsolicited—is one of the most difficult things you can do. It usually tests our ability to listen carefully. It often causes us to react defensively, rather than recognizing it as an opportunity for growth and as an opportunity to understand better how others see us.

When you receive constructive feedback, your first focus should be on understanding the feedback with which you are being provided. If you don't understand what the person is saying, ask for clarification or ask them to provide you with a specific example. Don't assume that you know what the person is saying or try to read between the lines. Use phrases such as these:

- "Would you give me an example of a time I...."
- "Help me understand what you mean by ___."

Use paraphrasing to check for understanding. Feedback will be of benefit only when you understand what the person is really saying (as opposed to what you *think* they are saying). After the person has given his or her feedback, paraphrase back what you understood them to say to make sure that what you thought the person said is what she or he actually said. You can use phrases such as these:

- "Let me see if I get what you are saying. It sounds like you're saying _____. Is that right?
- "So, in terms of _____, you're saying that I _____. Is that right?"

Don't try to explain your behavior or act defensively. Too often when we get constructive feedback, our urge is to either become defensive or to explain away the behavior ("I would have done it except...," "You don't understand...," "It's not what you think...," and so on). These types of responses do not help you objectively evaluate your performance, nor do they contribute to your personal growth. Simply accept that this person's perception of your behavior is real to them and no amount of explanation or defensiveness is going to change it.

Thank the person for their gift. Yes, their feedback is a gift to you. Recognize that it is difficult for most people to give us honest feedback in the first place. They want to give us honest feedback, but they don't want to hurt our feelings. The fact that someone is willing to give you honest feedback means that he or she trusts that you will accept the feedback in the spirit in which it is being given—to be helpful.

Finally, the most difficult part of accepting constructive feedback is doing an internal evaluation. Now that you have the facts and perceptions of the other person or people, it's time to look at the message that this feedback is sending you. This means looking at the feedback in terms of at least the following criteria:

- Am I hearing the same thing from other people?
- How is this feedback similar to or different from other feedback I've received?
- Is it possible that what this person has said is true/accurate?
- Is this the way I want to be perceived by others? If not, what behavioral changes are necessary?

5. Build Relationships

Sadly, most of us spend more time with the people with whom we work than we do with our family and friends. Now, you would think that when you spend that much time with a group of people, you would know practically everything there is to know about them. The reality is that most of us don't even know basic things about the person who works in the cubicle right next to us.

Building solid working relationships is critical to your personal success in the world of work. It can, however, be challenging to build and maintain those relationships when you're being pulled in a dozen different directions.

Regardless, you need to find—or make—time to build relationships across the organization if you expect to be successful at work. Your ability to relate well to, and work effectively with, others at work is critical. Recognize, though, that it takes time to build solid working relationships—sometimes even years, depending on a wide variety of factors.

Mac and Ann Overcome a Strained Working Relationship

Mac and Ann were both managers in the same department. After the fact, they found out that, from the beginning, the odds were stacked against them developing a good working relationship. The boss subtly shared negative information with each about the other, they were put on projects where they were competing for resources, they were given goals that ran counter to each other, and more.

Unfortunately, they allowed themselves to become unknowing victims. They managed to maintain a polite association for the good of the department and the organization, but that was the end of it. In a downsizing, Ann lost her job; four months later, Mac did too. The strained relationship continued to bother Ann, so she contacted Mac and arranged for them to have breakfast together.

Fast-forward three years. Ann and Mac aren't bosom buddies, but they do regularly keep in touch and have pretty much healed the wounds that never should have been.

When you take the time and make the effort to build positive relationships with your co-workers, you are more likely to enjoy your job and tend to be more productive. Remember, though, that it takes only one thoughtless action to destroy even well-healed working relationships.

To help build productive working relationships with others:

1. **Draw a line between being friendly and being too personal in your relationships.** Sharing the name of your co-worker's spouse and children is one thing; talking about the very personal fight you had with your spouse last night is another thing altogether. If the information that you share with your co-workers is too personal and intimate—by their standards—they are likely to try to avoid you so that they don't have to listen to your stories.

2. **People's perceptions are their realities.** Communication is not what you said or thought you said. Your actions are not what you mean them to be, but what they appear to be. You might do and say things that you intend to have one meaning (for example, helpful, beneficial, or innocuous), but others interpret it differently (for example, rude, undermining, or self-serving). The temptation in these situations is to discredit the other person's interpretation. *Resist that temptation.* Regardless of what you meant by your words or actions, recognize that my perception is my reality and nothing you can do is going to change that. All you can do is repair the broken bridge.

3. **Don't gossip about co-workers, bosses, customers, or anyone else in or associated with the company.** Yes, there are people who love gossip—other gossipers! People who gossip are rarely trusted. The thought on everyone's mind is, "If he/she is saying this about [person], what is he/she saying about me behind *my* back?" (See chapter 4 for more on dealing with gossiping co-workers.)

   Also remember the saying that "the walls have ears." Even things that you think are said in confidence, behind a closed door, will likely find a way of getting back to others.

4. **Treat others with respect.** Without this, it is virtually impossible to develop effective working relationships with others. Respect can take many forms, including

   - Actively listening to others

   - Being empathetic (not *sym*pathetic)

   - Not jumping to conclusions

   - Avoiding prejudice

   - Believing that everyone has something of value to contribute

5. **Keep your promises.** If you said that you would do something, you need to do it. People depend on you to deliver what you promise, when you promise it. Yes, there are times when emergencies and crises come up to foil the best-laid plans. When that happens, you need to get back to the people you committed to, let them know what happened, and work with them to resolve the conflict. That resolution might be a renegotiated timeframe, assistance, or many other things. The issue, though, is informing the people who are affected by your commitment so that they can make adjustments rather than experiencing last-minute surprises.

6. **Give credit where credit is due.** And, probably more importantly, don't take credit for work that you didn't do.

7. **Keep confidences.** If someone tells you something in confidence, it means that you do not—even by changing the names—share the story with anyone else. When you keep confidences, people come to trust you, which, in turn, contributes to positive working relationships.

8. **Offer to—and respond to requests to—help co-workers.** When you have—or can make—a little time, pitch in and help out. It's like putting money in the bank. If you help others when you have a few minutes, they will help you when you have an emergency.

9. **Keep your emotions under control.** Another person's inappropriate behavior or strong emotion is not a reason for you to respond in kind. As hard as it might be, you need to stay calm, cool, and collected. Your goal should be to understand *why* the person is reacting in such a way and—if it is an issue with you—work with the person to resolve it.

10. **Be honest.** No one appreciates dishonesty, even if you think you are being that way for a good reason. That doesn't mean that you should be brutally honest. Learn to be honest using tact and diplomacy.

11. **Take the blame when you deserve it.** It is never anyone else's fault that you didn't get something done, that you did something you shouldn't, that you let the team down, or anything else. You are the only person who is responsible for your behavior—no one else controls what you do.

    You have a choice: You can choose to let an obstacle stop you, or you can choose to take actions to remove the obstacle. When you are responsible for a breakdown, take responsibility for it. For example, "I'm sorry. I didn't write it down and I forgot about it. I will e-mail it to everyone before the end of the day today." This will go a lot further than pointing the finger of blame at someone or something else.

12. **Take the "two ears and one mouth" approach.** In other words, spend twice as much time learning about others' opinions, ideas, values, perspective, and so on as you do trying to get others to see things your way. Then, when it comes time for you to voice your personal opinions, ideas, values, perspectives, and so on, do it with tact and respect.

13. **Pick your battles.** There are some things that you should fight for, and there are times where winning the battle might result in you losing the war.

    Sometimes you need to give in on things that are minor, small, or inconsequential to you, but significant to the other person. Recognize that there will be a time when you need that person's support on something that is important to you. You'll be much more likely to get that support if you have already established a give-and-take relationship.

6. Share What You Know

"Knowledge is power" used to be a common philosophy that employees at all levels embraced. Unfortunately, there are still pockets of people who believe this. Today's revised credo, for the most part, is "Knowledge is power *when it is shared*." Effective team members share information, knowledge, skills, and experiences with others so that everyone's skills, abilities, and contributions are elevated. Some of the ways you can share include the following:

- If you are good at something, teach it to someone else.

- If you have knowledge that others don't, find at least one other person to share it with.

- Look for opportunities to pass along to new employees what you have learned about the company.

- If you went through an experience the same or similar to what someone else is going through, share the experience with him or her, along with what you learned.

7. Set an Example for Others on the Team

The list of ways to set a good example could go on for pages, but we'll assume that you're reading this for enlightenment rather than as a cure for insomnia. So, here's the short list, in the form of a checklist. The goal is to be able to check off each of these items.

Good Example Checklist

❏ Instead of complaining and whining about situations that can be improved, I take action to make improvements.

❏ I set an example by taking initiative rather than waiting for others to set something right.

❏ I don't try to dump my "dirty work" on others.

❏ I actively work to encourage functional conflict (conflict that helps the team get better) and resolve dysfunctional conflict (that which works against the effectiveness of the team).

❏ My team members would describe me as reliable. I can be counted on to consistently, and in a quality manner, get my work done, do my fair share, and follow through on assignments.

❏ My team members would consider me to be flexible—able to roll with the punches without getting stressed out or complaining.

❏ My team members would say that I am open to considering points of view and opinions that are different from my own and that I am willing to compromise when appropriate.

❏ Anyone who knows me would say I care about my work, my team, and the team's work.

❏ When I have decisions to make that will impact others, I make every effort to get their input before making the decision.

❏ I have a genuine interest in the work-related well-being of other team members.

❏ My team members would say that I value differences and see them as positive components of our diverse work team.

❏ I have a good, appropriate sense of humor that I use in both good and bad times.

❏ I take my responsibility as a team member seriously.

Now, if you want to really make it tough, ask your fellow team members to rate you on each of the statements, too. When they can honestly say that each of the statements is "true" about you, then you've really got something!

8. Be Adaptable and Flexible

Change is inevitable. We've all heard the cliché. Nowhere is it more evident than in the workplace. There are days where it seems like the direction of the company is 180 degrees different at the end of the day than it was in the morning. You get projects that go through multiple changes—and sometimes even disappear—before you're halfway through them. You finally get to the point that you understand what you job is and you're doing it well, and all of a sudden it changes.

It's easy to get frustrated in these kinds of situations and feel that the company's leadership doesn't have a clue about what they're doing. But digging in your heels and fighting change is ineffective. Success lies with the person who is able to quickly adapt to and support whatever is being changed (and it will be changed, regardless of how hard you or others fight it).

If you want to be seen as a team player who is flexible and adaptable to constant change, remember that

- Your willingness to be gracious and helpful when things change for the umpteenth time will earn you the reputation of being a team player.

- Your ability to realize that everything you enjoy now was a change to someone else will show that you understand the broader context of change.

- Your skills at rapidly recovering and moving on will show that you are able to align with the new environment.

- Your focus on ensuring operational improvements before, during, and after the change will show that you are a person with a bottom-line focus.

Get over feeling hurt, angry, frustrated, or whatever other emotion is stressing you out. Get over it and get on board. It's the person who moves beyond the personal implications of change and works for the positive organizational results who will be the one thriving through organizational change.

Now I've Got It, Right?

So, once you master these eight behaviors, you're set, right? Well, not necessarily. There are other important characteristics and behaviors such as integrity, honesty, compassion, loyalty, and optimism— just to mention a few—that are also important.

These are simply eight very important team member behaviors, and there are only so many things you can work on at one time. If you are able to master these eight behaviors, chances are, you're developing other important ones, too.

Conclusion: Work Toward Being a Team Player

"Plays well with others." It's a phrase from our kindergarten report card that is still a critical skill in today's workplace. It's not as easy as it used to be, though. Instead of just sharing your toys and not hitting others, you need to develop and effectively utilize the social skills to build productive working relationships. Hopefully this chapter has helped you to think about your areas of strength as a team player, identify your developmental opportunities, and start thinking about a plan for improvement.

Answers to the Exercise (Page 129)

1. **False.** Constructive feedback needs to be descriptive rather than evaluative. That means using "I" statements rather than

sending "you" messages. Feedback provided in this manner reduces the chance that the other person will respond defensively. It also allows the other person the freedom to use, or not use, the feedback as he or she sees fit. Say "During the meeting I noticed that you…" rather than "You shouldn't have done ____ during the meeting."

2. **False,** on two counts. First, the feedback needs to be specific rather than general. Say, "I get frustrated when you don't follow through on your commitments to the rest of the team…" instead of, "You're irresponsible." The second reason it's not good feedback is the use of the word "always." If you think about it, people are rarely consistently at extremes—always, never. These words, though, are sometimes added to show the speaker's exasperation with the situation or to emphasize the problem, even though they are rarely warranted. And they will almost always result in the recipient of the feedback reacting defensively (for example, "I do NOT always do that").

3. **True.** Constructive feedback should focus only on the current or present situation. Avoid bringing the past into the situation. The only thing that is important is what happened right here and now. The person can't change the past because, well… the past is the past. So, just leave the past alone. Say, "During the meeting this morning…" rather than "Just like during the last three meetings, this morning you…."

4. **False.** Constructive feedback should only be given in the amount the receiver can use, which might not necessarily coincide with the amount of information you would like to give. Although you want to be specific, you don't want to overload the person. This will decrease the possibility that the person will be able to—and will even want to—do something with and about the feedback.

5. **True.** Constructive feedback should be focused on the person's behaviors, not on the person. The focus of the feedback needs to be on something that the person has the ability to change or improve (a behavior, an action, or a skill), rather than something the person has no control over (for example, a personality trait). Say, "It really concerns me that you don't get the team involved in making more of the decisions…" rather than "You run this team like a dictator."

6. **False.** When providing feedback, speak for yourself, not for anyone else. If others feel the same way you do, they need to provide that feedback to the offending team member themselves, taking ownership of the impact the person's behavior has on them. Say, "I get distracted when you…" rather than, "Everyone on the team is distracted when you…."

7. **True.** Feedback that does not consider the needs of the feedback receiver and giver, is *de*structive rather than *con*structive. Feedback given to satisfy a personal need or desire, to make you feel better, or to gain a psychological advantage over the other person, is destructive and should not be given. Say, "I'm concerned that the team's meetings aren't as effective as they would be if we followed the agenda…" rather than "That meeting was a joke! If you don't learn how to run better meetings, I'm going to tell my boss I want off this useless team."

8. **False.** Of course, there is an exception to this, as there is to most rules. If there is absolutely, positively no way you can get the feedback to the person any sooner, give the feedback as soon thereafter as humanly possible. The rule of thumb to follow is that the closer the event and the feedback, the more relevance the feedback is perceived to have and the more value the receiver will place on it. When giving constructive feedback, though, you might need to factor your emotional state into the equation. For example, if you are really upset about what the person did (or didn't do) and are on the verge of an emotional outburst, it would be wise to give yourself some time to cool down before approaching the other person.

9. **False.** Constructive feedback is about sharing information rather than giving advice. When people receive feedback, they should be free to decide for themselves whether or not the information is valid, and whether or not to act on the information. If the feedback a person receives is not deemed to be valid or is not in line with his or her goals, needs, or values, it should not be incumbent upon the person to take action of any kind. We are all free to decide what to do with any kind of information we receive.

PART 3

Skills for Getting Ahead

CHAPTER 7

Tapping into the Positive Side of Conflict Situations

A conflict is any situation in which the interests of two or more people appear to be incompatible. Conflict is also a process that is triggered when one person believes that someone else is presenting a barrier to meeting his or her goals. Conflicts can occur with co-workers, your boss, people who work for you, higher-level company executives, or customers. This chapter explores the nature of conflict at work, as well as how to resolve conflicts to everyone's advantage. The following short story provides an example of a conflict at work.

Carol Is Stunned by a Lack of Cooperation and Loses Her Cool

Having been employed for nine months, Carol was accustomed to the routine of the biweekly staff meeting. All staff members were expected to come prepared to give a two- to three-minute update, to include recent successes, key issues to be resolved, and requests for assistance from others. During her turn, Carol shared information about the company's upcoming open house for employees' families and the need for people to assist with check-in and the running of various activities. She had been unsuccessfully requesting help for a month and was very concerned because the open house was in just a few days.

The initial reaction of the other staff members to Carol's plea included looking down to avoid eye contact, reading their papers, or commenting about how shorthanded they are. Then Jack stated, "I have important production deadlines that affect this company more than

(continued)

(continued)

your open house. I don't even know why we are doing this now during our busy season." Andrea said, "I agree. This is the worst time of year for an open house. Most of the people in my department aren't having their families come anyway."

Before anyone else could join in, Carol angrily responded, "All of you were at the meeting when we agreed on this date. At that time each of you said you would provide people to help. I need one person from each of you, or the open house will be cancelled because you were unable to help." In response to this statement, everyone started speaking at once.

Types of Conflict

Even though there are many types of conflicts, most situations can fit into one of the following four categories:

- Differences and incompatibility
- Scarcity of resources
- Interpersonal issues
- A high-stress work environment

Differences and Incompatibility

When you interact with people at work, often what you notice most are the ways that people are different from you. These differences include experiences, opinions, and work style. The natural tendency is to see and focus on ways these differences are disadvantageous to you. So, people tend to gravitate toward and feel more comfortable with others who are similar to them. This tendency reinforces the negative aspects of the differences.

The irony is that these differences can lead to better results because of the creativity that can arise when you listen and are open to learning from others. Instead of letting differences be roadblocks to working with others, you should deliberately explore differences. By doing so, you open your mind to new approaches that can improve your results. Exploring differences requires humility, an interest in learning, and courage.

Incompatibility at work occurs when one's interests and needs are inconsistent or at odds with someone else's interests and needs. For example, your career interests might be inconsistent with what your boss has in mind for you. Or, you might want to try something new, while your co-workers want to maintain the status quo. These types of conflicts can result in stalemates, or working around the other person.

Scarcity of Resources

A scarcity of resources occurs when there is a limited availability of people, money, equipment, or space, which causes people to fight for these resources to help themselves or their departments achieve their goals. This type of conflict can occur during the budgeting process when department heads with normally good relationships become rivals for limited funds. Or, during high-volume times of the year, a department may request to "borrow" people from other departments. There is hesitancy to loan out these people, who might in fact be available, because of the fear of not getting them back. This conflict leads to unnecessary spending and wasted resources for the overall company. Or, the marketing department might have been allocated funding for Project A, determined to be a top priority. Six months into the year, a key executive is replaced, and the new person places Project A on the back burner, replacing it with Project A-plus, to be completed on quick timing by the finance department. Because funds were not allocated to finance, they need to make a case to receive a transfer of funds from the marketing department. How do you think the marketing department will respond to this potential loss of funds?

Interpersonal Issues

Conflicts due to interpersonal issues include rivalries and the dislike of other individuals. These issues can lead to some of the most uncomfortable conflicts amongst people. Interpersonal issues often become worse when one person complains about another to their friends at work, instead of speaking directly to the other person. The "rival" hears about it and either confronts the complainer or stirs the pot further by finding a way to retaliate. Many times this type of conflict is a result of inadequate two-way communication— not taking the time to explain *and* listen to understand the source of the rivalry (see chapter 6 for more on improving communication). Or, the dislike of the other person might be due to an unwillingness to invest time in developing a trusting professional relationship. This unwillingness might be due to a preconceived bias about the other person. Gaining someone's trust requires time and a series of positive experiences. Dislike of a co-worker can be unproductive if you start out disliking an individual and continue to be closed-minded despite attempts by the other person to build trust.

A High-Stress Work Environment

A stressful environment can cause people to lash out at others due to the constant pressure that they experience. When employees feel overburdened with their workload, they do not take the time that is needed to work through issues in a healthy manner. In addition to feeling mounting pressure, one's patience wanes during times of stress, which leads to an unhealthy approach to conflict. Instead of seeking to understand others' views, when you are stressed you tend to push to get your own agenda and preferences met. Conflict results when others with different preferences are also pushing aggressively.

Understanding Conflict

Conflict situations can be especially challenging when you are relatively young, new to the organization, or have not yet gained the respect that comes with experience. To begin understanding conflict better, try answering the questions in the following exercise for a recent conflict situation you experienced at work.

Exercise: Insights into a Recent Conflict

1. What were the causes of the conflict?

   _____

   _____

2. How did you and the other(s) involved react? What were you thinking and feeling?

   _____

   _____

   _____

3. What were the positive and negative outcomes of the conflict?

   _____

   _____

   _____

4. How did you feel about the situation at the time, and how do you feel about it now?

_____

_____

_____

Too often, in the midst of conflict, and even immediately after, most people don't think about and reflect on what happened. It is important to take time to identify what you can learn from your approach, the other person's reaction to you, and your reaction to the other person. Doing so can help build trust and improve your response during the next conflict. For example, in a recent conflict, perhaps you thought about saying some things but decided not to in fear of the reaction that you anticipated. Next time, you could try stating the facts in a neutral way and following them with a question. In the story at the beginning of this chapter, Carol could have said in a matter-of-fact tone, "Every department head agreed to provide one person each to help with the open house activities. I have names for three of the seven departments, so I need four more people. What ideas do you have on how we can fulfill this need?" This would have set the stage for a more factual and less emotional discussion about the next steps.

Or, in your recent conflict situation maybe you didn't understand the points that the other person made, but you didn't try to find out because you didn't want to appear uninformed. Next time, try asking clarifying questions that will inform you and also show your interest in the other person's ideas. If others are involved, they might have the same questions and appreciate you asking. Some examples of clarifying questions include the following:

- How did you arrive at that conclusion?
- What might be the impact of that decision?
- What are the advantages of that option?
- Who was involved?

The Benefits of Conflict

Most people tend to think of conflict in a negative way. This response is natural because the word is regularly used to describe violence and wars. It can be productive to reframe conflict as positive and look for the value and benefits from the situation. Review your answer to question 3 in the exercise on page 146. It might have been difficult for you to see any positive outcomes of the conflict. As you read the following list of the benefits of conflict, try to identify which benefits could have been potential outcomes of your recent conflict situation.

- Developing productive work relationship(s)
- Improving communication
- Reducing frustration
- Increasing creativity
- Increasing job satisfaction

It can be difficult to figure out how to achieve the benefits of conflict because you naturally become tied up with the emotions that you feel during the conflict and the fallout after the conflict. Some specific ways to achieve each of the benefits follow in table 7.1.

Table 7.1: Ways to Achieve the Benefits of Conflict

Benefit	Ways to Achieve the Benefit
Developing productive work relationships	Instead of focusing on differences and incompatibilities, actively search for commonalities. Then, look for chances to discuss the interests that you have in common with the other individual(s).
	A few days after an especially difficult conflict, ask the other person(s) for time to discuss what happened. Share your perspectives and ask for theirs. Together, identify possible ways to handle future disagreements so that you can both feel satisfied.
Improving communication	Whenever possible, share any concerns you have directly with the others.
	Avoid talking or complaining about others while at work. If you need to vent, do your venting away from work. Talking through the situation with a neutral third person can help clarify issues and put them in perspective. This then can prepare you to have a productive discussion with the other person(s).

Benefit	Ways to Achieve the Benefit
Reducing frustration	When an issue is blocking your progress on a project, promptly address the issue.
	When you are hesitant to share a concern, plan out your approach. Think through how the other person might react, and ways you could respond professionally.
Increasing creativity	When you hear an idea or opinion that is different than yours, instead of focusing on why it won't work, ask questions and listen for how it might work. Look for something positive in the idea.
	Build on others' ideas, instead of immediately knocking them down.
Increasing job satisfaction	As conflicts arise, use your communication skills to resolve the conflict by actively listening and clarifying the true issues.
	After a conflict situation, identify ways to learn and grow from the situation. Set goals for reaping the benefits in future conflicts.

Discovering Your Strengths and Weaknesses in Handling Conflict

You most likely have a preferred way of dealing with conflict situations. For example, when someone in authority has an opinion you disagree with, you might prefer to keep your thoughts to yourself rather than engage in a discussion. Or, you might enjoy engaging in a lively argument and investigation of all sides of an issue. Perhaps you want to try to please and accommodate others. In fact, you might put your interests behind those of others. Or, during conflict you might try to reach a middle ground. These approaches are just four examples of ways to handle conflict. By completing the statements in the exercise on page 150, you can gain insights into your preferred approach to conflict, and your strengths and weaknesses.

Exercise: Understanding Your Approach to Conflict

1. A time I felt good about how I dealt with a conflict at work was when…

   _____

   _____

   _____

2. The reasons I felt positive about this situation were that I…

   _____

   _____

   _____

3. When someone disagrees with me about something important to me, I usually…

   _____

   _____

   _____

4. When someone challenges me in front of others, I usually…

   _____

   _____

   _____

5. When someone avoids conflict with me, I normally…

   _____

   _____

   _____

6. My challenges in handling conflict include…

   _____

   _____

   _____

As you look at Juanita's answers, you will gain new insights about Juanita. Identify what you see as her strengths and weaknesses.

Juanita's Answers to the Questions

1. A time I felt good about how I dealt with a conflict at work was when I helped resolve a conflict between two co-workers in a meeting. They were in disagreement about how to present their team's recommendations. I saw how their ideas were compatible and was able to suggest a way to use the ideas from each of them. This resulted in a more interesting and compelling presentation, and ownership by both people.

2. The reason I felt positive about this situation was that I was new to the team and to this point had been pretty quiet. So, I was glad I was able to make a contribution because I had been listening intently during the meeting.

3. When someone disagrees with me about something important to me, I tend to get quiet. I need time to think. Also, I don't particularly like arguing with team members.

4. When someone challenges me in front of others, I tend to shrink further, which can negatively affect my credibility with others.

5. When someone avoids conflict with me, I normally empathize because I also am uncomfortable with conflict. I tend to make the first move by asking a question and then listening and learning about the other person's issues and opinions.

6. My challenges in handling conflict include my discomfort with it and my need to think through the issues before responding.

Juanita's answers provide insights about both her strengths and her weaknesses. One of her strengths is her ability to actively listen to others and develop more creative solutions than others who might not be listening as closely. Juanita's area to improve is her discomfort with conflict and thus her tendency to avoid it.

Just as you evaluated Juanita's answers, take a moment to reflect on your answers to the six questions in the exercise on page 150 and identify both your strengths and weaknesses.

Using Your Strengths

One way you can improve your effectiveness is by understanding and fully utilizing your strengths. Too often, individuals just focus on trying to improve on their weaknesses. Although doing so is important, you don't want to overlook a chance to deliberately focus on making a positive impact with those traits that come naturally to you. Table 7.2 shows five examples of strengths that can be used during conflict. Find your strength, and read the ways to use it. Then, identify a specific opportunity at work when you can focus on using the strength.

Table 7.2: Using Your Strengths in Conflict Situations

Strength	Ways to Use Your Strength
Active listening	When others are arguing their positions with you, learn how their positions overlap with your thinking on the issue. Then, make a proposal that reflects the overlaps in the positions.
Able to clearly explain others' concerns	In group settings, clarify others' positions to help the entire group become clearer about each person's intended point.
Team player	Let go of your solution as the only possible way, and explore the reasons behind others' positions.
Risk taker	When an argument continues without progress, redirect the discussion to dig further to reveal the real issue. Ask everyone involved for the reasons for their preferences. Doing so can lead to the development of new solutions.
Comfortable bringing issues forward to your boss	Coach others who are more hesitant to speak with the boss and practice by role-playing with them.

Working on Your Weaknesses

There is also value in working on your weaknesses. To maximize your effectiveness at work, you must address your challenges and barriers. If you don't address your weaknesses, you might find that others try to avoid you during conflict because you are abrasive. Or if you seem uncomfortable with disagreements, they will not involve you.

Some ideas for addressing behaviors that can inhibit your ability to influence others are shown in table 7.3. Look in the first column in to find your area of weakness. As you did with your strengths, think of a specific time at work when you can put to use the suggestions in the middle column. The last column provides the motivation for improving.

Table 7.3: Addressing Negative Behaviors

Instead of	Try	Because You Will
Avoiding the conflict	Sharing your opinion and the reasons why you feel that way, using a neutral, matter-of-fact tone. Asking others their thoughts on the issue.	■ Increase your credibility with others ■ Resolve issues before they become unmanageable
Putting down the other person	Asking a clarifying question or building on others' ideas. Always staying on the high ground.	■ Work toward a more productive work relationship ■ Reap more creative solutions
Putting aside your concerns to satisfy others	Being clear and specific in sharing your ideas and opinions. Using examples that others understand.	■ Gain respect from others ■ Have a greater impact on others ■ Feel better about your job
Focusing on winning the conflict through strong arguments	Looking for mutual gains for all sides and listening for common interests. Stating your feelings in a nonjudgmental manner.	■ Reach a more optimal solution ■ Experience a smoother implementation of the solution
Simply looking for the middle ground	Building on the current thinking to discover new possibilities.	■ Attain a solid long-term solution ■ Increase everyone's level of satisfaction with the solution

Case Studies of Conflict Situations

Now that you know more about your own conflict-management style, let's see how you might put what you've learned to use in a variety of real situations. For each of these scenarios, you will read background information and possible options that the individual might choose to handle the situation. You might also think of alternative actions. After reading each situation, try deciding which response is ideal.

Situation One: Audrey's Boss Is Averse to New Ideas and Change

Audrey had been in her job for about 10 months when she suggested to her boss that they try a new approach with a client's semi-annual fund-raiser. Her boss responded that the client had always liked what was done in the past, so she didn't want to change it. Audrey explained why she thought the client would like the improvement, and listened while her boss told her to focus on executing her plan instead of trying to be creative. Her boss had made this comment to Audrey in previous conversations when she had made improvement suggestions on other projects. What should Audrey do next?

1. Say nothing and return to her cubicle in frustration.

2. Quit her job and go to an employer who appreciates creativity and is open to change.

3. Use her new approach anyway with the client's fund-raiser, and worry about telling her boss later.

4. Talk with her boss's boss about the idea and try to get his support.

5. Talk to the boss the next day. Bring data that justifies how the change will better meet the client's desires. Create a detailed plan that shows how the change will not require any additional cost, nor delay the timeline.

Audrey might end up with option 2, but it is best for her to first try option 5 with her boss. It sounds like her boss might be averse to risk, wanting to avoid failures. For both the organization and for Audrey, this can result in stagnation and a loss of creativity over time. Providing the boss with some additional facts and a detailed plan might help the boss become more comfortable with trying something different. If Audrey senses that there is still hesitation, she can be prepared to suggest a modification to her plan, which includes some of what is currently done. If the boss stays closed-minded, Audrey might want to beef up both her resume and her networking.

Situation Two: Dana Feels She Is Overdue for a Raise

Dana has worked for the same company for 2½ years. She automatically received raises at her 6-month, 12-month, and 18-month anniversaries with the company. It has now been 12 months since her last raise. Dana is upset about this delay but not sure what to do about it because her relationship with her boss is a bit shaky. She has worked for him for 1½ years and still doesn't feel at ease talking with him. The idea of asking for a raise has her losing sleep. Which of these options do you suggest for Dana?

1. Wait it out. Life is too stressful without adding more stress.

2. Bite the bullet. During her next scheduled meeting with her boss, Dana should explain how long it has been and ask why she has gone so long without a raise.

3. Go to the human resources department and ask confidentially how frequently she should expect to receive raises.

4. Practice asking for a raise with her friend, and the next day ask the boss whether he has time to meet. After sharing when the last increase occurred, she can ask how raises are determined and when she might expect another one.

5. Go into the boss's office demanding a raise and threatening to quit if it isn't high enough or quick enough.

Although option 5 is one you might have fantasized about, it is better to discuss the pay situation with your boss informally, after practicing what to say (option 4). One key is to ask questions using a neutral voice tone without attacking, whining, or showing negative emotions such as anger. Also, be prepared to ask a follow-up question to a response you might not want to hear. For example, Dana's boss might respond by telling her "Don't worry, you are doing just fine and you will get a raise when it makes sense." Then Dana can say "Thank you for that reassurance. It would be helpful for me to understand how raises are determined. When can we arrange a time for you to review that with me?" You will find that a professional approach gets the best results.

Situation Three: John's Proposal Is Shot Down

The use of electronic communication saves time and money. Yet the words on the screen or on the printed page can take on a meaning that the sender did not intend. Also, because the message can be read multiple times, the reader might give more significance to it than the sender intended.

John was on a team working to complete a project important to the rest of the department. At the end of the last team meeting, he volunteered to draft a proposal for the rest of the team to review. Everyone had agreed to this approach because it was a timesaver and it would be much easier to have a document to react to than to have all eight team members work together to draft something from scratch. John e-mailed the proposal to all the team members.

Within minutes of having sent the e-mail, John and the rest of the team received a message back from Craig, another team member known as a chronic troublemaker. Craig's scathing e-mail ripped John's proposal to pieces. Craig's final sentence was "John has gone against everything that the committee has discussed, so his proposal is worthless to us. We need to start over." John was in shock while reading the e-mail. His best next step is to:

1. Immediately hit "reply all" and send back his opinion of Craig and his e-mail, explaining where Craig can put it.

2. Send an e-mail to the head of the committee telling her he is quitting.

3. Forward the e-mail to Craig's boss, explaining that this is an example of why it is so difficult to work with Craig.

4. Print the e-mail and bring it with him as he leaves for the day. It is now after 6:00 p.m., anyway.

5. Meet with Craig after receiving input from the rest of the team. Give Craig feedback on the inappropriate nature of his message and find out what Craig's specific issue is with the proposal.

Options 4 and 5 combined make sense for John. It is important for John to deal with the e-mail message with Craig, but not today, and not via e-mail. John needs time to calm down and plan his approach with Craig, who thrives on stirring up trouble. It is important that John doesn't lower himself to Craig's level. When he speaks with

Craig, John needs to utilize "I" messages (see chapter 4, "Dealing with Difficult Co-workers"). It is also important for John to hear balanced feedback about his draft from other committee members. These perspectives will help him speak with Craig without being overly defensive or emotional. Finally, the idea of sending the draft was to get input. Craig might in fact have valid concerns, but doesn't know how to communicate them professionally. By asking Craig questions, John can get to the root issue.

Strategies for Handling Conflict Situations

Table 7.4 summarizes some workplace conflicts you might encounter and suggests strategies for each.

Table 7.4: Strategies for Handling Conflict Situations

Situation	Strategy
You want to influence someone who generally prefers the status quo to utilize a new approach.	■ Share data that justifies how the change will better meet the customer's needs. ■ Create a detailed plan that addresses objections and concerns. ■ Garner support from others who have influence.
You need to bring up an important issue that causes you to feel uncomfortable, such as asking your boss for a raise, or telling a co-worker that he or she has a hygiene problem.	■ Plan what you will say, keeping in mind the other person's strengths and weaknesses in dealing with conflict. ■ Brief a friend on the situation and practice possible realistic scenarios. ■ Use a neutral tone of voice to make your points and ask questions in a matter-of-fact manner.
You need to follow up with an individual who inappropriately lashed out at you front of others.	■ Calm down and get your emotions under control before reacting to the other person. ■ Plan your words and practice, practice, practice. ■ Meet with the individual as soon as you have completed the first two bullets. Stay on the high ground—don't stoop to the other person's level.

(continued)

(continued)

Situation	Strategy
	■ Use the "I" message approach using neutral body language and voice tone. ■ Keep any negative feelings about the person separate from the discussion.
During a meeting, you are once again in disagreement with another team member. You consistently see the same situation in totally different ways, and have different ideas about solutions and next steps.	■ Instead of focusing on your argument and the points you want to convey, actively listen to hear the meaning and intent of the other person's viewpoints. ■ Identify ways to build on the other person's ideas. ■ Listen for commonalities in your viewpoints, and work from there.
You are surprised when a colleague approaches you and shares concerns about how you treated him or her.	■ Before responding, listen and ask non-accusatory questions to ensure that you understand the person's message. ■ Thank your colleague for coming to you with the concern. ■ If you were in the wrong, say so and apologize. If you believe your actions were appropriate, still thank the individual and sincerely say that you will think about what was shared.

Group Conflict Resolution

Most of the examples in this chapter have been about conflicts with one other person. Yet, the techniques discussed also apply to group resolution of conflict. In addition to these techniques, it is helpful to use a group process to deal with conflict more productively. As you gain more confidence in these skills, you can take a leadership role in resolving group conflicts following the process discussed here. The group process involves the following steps:

1. Identify and agree to ground rules for the discussion.

2. Clearly define the issue or problem and criteria for making the decision.

3. Brainstorm possible approaches and options for addressing the issue or problem.

4. Discuss the pros and cons of each option.

5. Make a group decision using the agreed-upon criteria.

6. Evaluate the group's process.

Step 1: Identify and Agree to Ground Rules for the Discussion

By using ground rules, the group has a better chance of maintaining professional standards of behavior during the discussion. With these standards, it will be easier to focus on the issues and not be distracted by inappropriate behavior. When all group members participate in developing ground rules, there is more ownership in them and a greater chance of following them.

When you see that the group is in the early stages of conflict, suggest that they take 5 to 10 minutes to develop ground rules. Suggest one or two statements to get the group started. Examples that have worked well for other groups include the following:

- One person speaks at a time.

- Be open-minded to other viewpoints.

- Listen actively to others' opinions and the rationale for their opinions.

- Balance airtime to ensure that everyone gets a chance to participate in the discussions.

- Use your creativity to build on others' ideas and come up with new possibilities.

- Stay constructive when expressing opinions, without making personal attacks on others.

Step 2: Clearly Define the Issue or Problem and Criteria for Making the Decision

Often there appears to be a conflict because people are defining the issue differently, but are not aware of this difference. To avoid wasting time trying to solve multiple problems, first clarify the primary problem that needs to be addressed. In the introductory example of this chapter, Carol's issue was the gathering of additional open house volunteers, whereas Jack's issue was the timing of the open house.

Once you agree on the problem to be addressed, define the problem in specific terms and keep the statement concise. Example problem and issue statements include the following:

- Employee lateness has risen to an unacceptable level.
- Prospective clients are not accepting our proposals.
- Customer complaints due to unfriendly and unknowledgeable associates have doubled in the last month.

Once the problem statement is finalized, and before discussing the problem, establish criteria for deciding on a solution. This discussion might become heated, yet it needs to occur at this point to help direct and guide your group's decision. For example, a leadership team with responsibility for recommending employees for promotion each quarter struggled with its process until they agreed to a set of criteria. Once the criteria were established, the decision process went quickly and smoothly.

The nature of the issue will help guide your criteria selection. In addition to generic criteria, you will most likely have criteria that are specific to your issue. For example, the leadership team mentioned earlier established promotion criteria that addressed specific contributions and behaviors.

Some generic examples of criteria include the following:

- The solution must be doable and realistic with the current work environment and available resources.
- The solution can be implemented in a timely manner.
- The solution eliminates the root cause of the issue.
- The solution does not create new problems.

Step 3: Brainstorm Possible Approaches and Options for Addressing the Issue or Problem

When you brainstorm, you need to suspend all evaluation—both criticism and praise. This suspension of evaluation fosters creativity, yet it can be difficult to do. When you hear a new idea, it is natural to think of what might go wrong. Or, if you hear an idea you especially like, your tendency is to stop the creative process. So, brainstorming requires deliberate discipline.

To reinforce the suspension of all evaluation, use a fun method to gently remind people when they are evaluating. Options include hitting the ringer on a call bell when someone uses a "killer phrase" or gently tossing a six-inch-diameter foam ball toward the person who is criticizing an idea.

In addition to suspending evaluation, another essential aspect of brainstorming is to build on others' ideas. When a seemingly crazy idea is built upon and refined, it can become the perfect solution to a persistent problem. For this reason, actively encourage each person to contribute offbeat ideas that they might feel hesitant to offer the group.

Step 4: Discuss the Pros and Cons of Each Option

If your list of possible options numbers more than about five or six, narrow down the list by first combining similar options. When combining ideas, be careful not to lose the essence of the ideas. If you feel you are losing the core meaning, don't combine the ideas.

Next, use a voting process. One technique frequently used is to divide the total number of options by three and give each person that number of votes. For example, if after combining options there are 12 remaining, each person can vote for four (12 divided by 3) different options using the agreed-upon criteria from step two. Continue this voting technique until you have five or six options to discuss thoroughly. Before beginning the discussion, challenge group members to contribute the pros of options they disagree with, and the cons of their favorite options. This approach opens people up to considering all options and other possible combinations.

Step 5: Make a Group Decision Using the Agreed-Upon Criteria

One person begins by making a recommendation based on the previous analysis and discussion, and then tests for consensus. If everyone can support the decision, the group is done with this step. If there is disagreement, those who cannot support the decision are responsible for offering another solution that reflects previous discussions and the group's criteria.

Step 6: Evaluate the Group's Process

Too often teams skip this step, grateful that the decision is finally made. This final step reinforces continuous improvement of the team's decision-making process. First, honestly review the team's ground rules. Have each person identify what he or she would like the group to do the same and to do differently during the next team decision. Then, after the decision has been implemented, assess how well it met the criteria and addressed the issue or problem.

Although this group process for conflict resolution might seem lengthy and arduous, in the end it results in more successful conflict resolution because solid decisions are fully supported, and group members feel better during and after the conflict. The more this process is used, the more natural and streamlined it becomes.

Conclusion: Key Points to Remember About Conflict

- Accept that conflict is a way of life. Look for ways to reap the benefits and take on a positive role in conflict situations.

- Be prepared for conflict, thinking through others' possible objections to your ideas and ways to respond to them.

- Keep in mind your strengths, and look for chances to use them when dealing with conflict.

- Be aware of your normal way of responding to conflict situations. Take some risk and experiment with different responses. Assess whether your results improve with the new approaches.

- There are many ways people are different. These differences can result in conflict. Spending time understanding the differences will result in more productive conflict and more creative results.

- When in the midst of heated conflicts, stay calm and ensure that you are professional in your response to others. If necessary, take time to cool down before reacting.

- Use active listening skills to identify commonalities and build creative solutions.

- When you experience conflict in group settings, use a process for helping the group be more productive and effective.

CHAPTER 8 Influencing Others

Today, every person's job requires the ability to influence others in order to be successful. This applies to presidents as well as it does to janitors—and everyone in between. You may want to influence your boss to give you a raise (or a larger raise), a co-worker to provide you with some information, or a cross-functional team member to support an idea you have. You might have even influenced others to buy you lunch or cover for you when you skipped a meeting. Regardless of whom you need to influence, or for what purpose, being a skilled influencer will make your job easier.

What Is Influencing?

Influencing is simply a person's ability to consistently, ethically, legally, and morally gain support for his or her views and opinions in a way that preserves or builds the relationship with another individual, a group, or the organization.

Influencing is, in the end, a core competency for today's worker that is used on a day-to-day basis for negotiations, formal and informal presentations, building work relationships, getting tasks and projects completed, and managing upward—or managing your boss, which is sometimes necessary.

Table 8.1 demonstrates the characteristics of influencing, as opposed to the negative ways many people try to influence others at work.

Table 8.1: Characteristics of Influencing

Influencing Is About...	Rather Than...
Gaining support for your proposed course of action	Forcing, coercing, or cajoling compliance
Developing working relationships	Getting your own way
Achieving your desired result through your ability to listen, communicate, and gain support	Forcing your views on the others
Presenting your views and recommendations in a way that will win others over	Forcing others to do things your way
Presenting a clear, concise, convincing case for adopting/pursuing your recommendations	Trying to prove others wrong
Balancing being assertive and being responsive to others	Being aggressive and irresponsible
Moving your preferred agenda forward with the support and cooperation of others	Moving your agenda forward by pushing, forcing, or demanding cooperation or compliance from others

What Is Your Influencing Style?

Read through the following influencing style statements. Mark any of the statements that you believe are typical of you at work.

To Influence Others, I...

- ❑ Use my emotions (for example, get upset, threaten, yell) to get the cooperation I want or need.
- ❑ Manipulate them without them knowing; pretend to involve them and listen to what they have to say and how they feel.
- ❑ Pester or bug the other person until he or she finally gives in.
- ❑ Appeal to their loyalty to me or our friendship (for example, "Hey, we've been friends for a long time. Just do this one thing for me").
- ❑ Flatter them; compliment them and butter them up.
- ❑ Use promises of *quid pro quo* (for example, "Do this for me now, and later I will do something for you").

❏ Play office politics.

❏ Present the facts in ways that are most supportive of my perspective, sometimes overlooking information that doesn't help me make my case.

❏ Pout, withdraw, or act depressed until I get the "sympathy vote."

❏ Ignore the person who doesn't support me and proceed, knowing that eventually the person will realize that my way was and is the best way.

❏ Use co-workers I'm friends with or who owe me favors to help pressure someone into going along with me.

❏ Interpret any minimally applicable policy, procedure, or rule in a way that will get the other person to support my approach.

❏ Use negative consequences (for example, "If you don't do this, I will do this thing that you don't want me to do" or "If you don't do this, I'll get even by making your life miserable by _____").

❏ Find the moral aspect of the issue and get the person to agree based on those issues—regardless of how tangentially related the moral belief is to the issue or problem.

❏ Use the other's person's known propensity toward compassion (for example, "I'm really in a corner on this and I need your help").

Hopefully you made it through the list without checking any of the items. Each of those "influencing" styles is controlling, demanding, or both. Although these behaviors will probably get you immediate short-term action and results, the long-term losses are greater. These behaviors almost always result in

- A deterioration of teamwork

- Potentially irreparable damage to the other person's trust in you

- A loss of your credibility

- A lack of willingness of others to involve you in problem-solving or other decisions

- The other individual developing a negative impression of you, making it more difficult (if not impossible) for you to work with the person in the future

On the other hand, using effective influencing skills will almost always result in

- A better working relationship with the other person
- A higher level of commitment to the planned action
- An increase in the amount of respect the other person has for you
- A more timely resolution to the issue or problem
- A win-win outcome to the issue or problem
- A higher probability that the solution or action will be effective
- A higher level of trust

Seven Steps to Effective Influencing

This chapter walks you through a seven-step process for effective influencing:

Step 1: Research and Plan Your Approach

Step 2: Ascertain Readiness to Proceed

Step 3: Describe the Situation and Its Impact

Step 4: Explain Your Recommended Action

Step 5: Ask for the Person's Input

Step 6: Gain the Person's Support to Move Forward

Step 7: Implement and Review the Success of the Approach Taken

Step 1: Research and Plan Your Approach

Most people don't feel a need to spend more than a few minutes researching and planning their approach. Some people believe that because you can't predict what the other person is going to say or do, any time spent planning is a waste of time. They believe that the best approach is to jump right into meeting with the person as soon as you know that there is an issue or problem to be addressed and what you want done. After all, these people rationalize, "I know what I need/want from the other person, so why delay?"

The reason to delay is simple: If you want to be successful in your influencing, in a shorter period of time, and in a way that will preserve or enhance your relationship with the other person or group, you need to spend some of your time upfront doing the following:

- Planning and researching the situation

- Gaining a better understanding of the person or group you need to influence so that you know what is of value to the person or group

- Getting your information and facts organized

Unfortunately, there is no nice, neat formula that you can follow every single time to research and plan your approach. However, you might want to ask yourself questions that fall into the following categories:

- Background

- Goals and objectives

- The other person/group

- The informal organization

- Planning the meeting

You might not need to answer every question for every influencing situation, but the more you can answer, the more likely you are to go into the influencing situation confident and come out successful.

Background

Unless you understand the history and extent of the situation, it's almost impossible to present a solid case for the impact of the situation and the need to address it. The important focus here is on gathering the relevant facts. You're not looking for a person to blame; instead, you're looking for the information and data you can use to develop a solution so that the problem does not occur again. The following questions will help you prepare to start your influencing with an understanding of the entire situation.

1. What are the facts behind the situation?

   - When did it happen?

   - What caused it to happen (or contributed to it happening)?

   - How many times has it happened?

   - Over what time period has it happened?

   - What is the effect on the team/department/company?

2. What evidence can you provide that the problem exists and what is the extent of the problem?

3. What is likely to happen if the current situation is not addressed?

   - How did you come to that conclusion?

   - What facts or evidence do you have to support that conclusion?

4. What are the top three supporting arguments/facts you can provide to the person or group to influence them to support what you want?

5. What additional supporting arguments/facts might you want/need to use to establish your case?

Goals and Objectives

Your next step in planning is determining your desired end result or solution to the problem. Because you did your research, you now have enough of an understanding of the problem—and the facts surrounding it—to determine what you believe to be the best solution to the problem. It's important to recognize that, as you begin planning the influencing process, your solution might not end up being the best (for example, due to the other person having information you didn't have access to), or that you might be unable to get complete cooperation from the other person/group for your solution. Because of this, you also need to think about your fallback plan; that is, you need to know what less action or different kind of a solution you are willing to accept. Use the following questions to help determine this information:

1. What is your desired goal?

2. How will this solve the problem?

3. What is the minimum you are willing/able to accept (your fallback position)?

4. What do you want/need the other person or group to do?

   - What benefit will the person or group realize from doing what you want/need?

The Other Person/Group

Too often people look at influencing as something they do to the other person. However, if you take the time to gain an understanding—or better understanding—of the other person, it increases the likelihood that your communication during the influencing process will address that person's values, style, communication, and information needs. The more you can customize your communication to the other person, the more likely you are to be successful. Use these questions to help you gain an understanding of the other person.

1. What does the person's/group's work area tell you about his/her/their interests, values, and beliefs?

2. What do you know about the person/group?

   - How can you use what you know about him/her/them to connect to the person(s) to get him/her/them to buy into— or at least listen to—what you have to say?

3. What concerns might the person/group you are trying to influence have?

   - How might you be able to address these concerns?

4. What kind of data would be most helpful in influencing this person or group?

   - What way of presenting the data would be most accepted (for example, tables, color charts, text, or verbal)?

5. What can you do to make what you have to say relevant and important to the other person?

6. What are the negative issues you need to be upfront and honest with the other person/group about?

7. What are you going to do (reaction and action) if the person/group rejects your request or suggestion?

8. What, specifically, do you need from the person (or each person in the group or the group as a whole)?

9. How will you benefit from the person/group doing what you want?

10. What do you think the other person/group will want in terms of benefits or other outcomes?

    - What additional benefits or benefit enhancements could you offer?

11. What are the costs of the person/group doing what you want them to do?

    - What ways can you reduce these costs?

12. What might make it difficult for the person/group to do what you want?

   ■ What can you do to eliminate or reduce the difficulty?

13. What might you be willing and able to do to make it more likely for the person/group to agree to do what you want/need?

14. How will you approach the conversation to get their interest right away?

   ■ What issues/concerns of theirs will be addressed by their helping/supporting you?

   ■ What words will be most effective?

15. Who else will benefit from this being solved, and how?

   ■ How might you involve them in the discussion and/or solution?

16. What objections might they come up with?

   ■ How will you overcome these objections?

The Informal Organization

Sometimes the informal organization (the way employees network with each other as opposed to the way the company is formally structured) has more power to change things in the organization than you could ever hope to muster through the formal channels of the organization's hierarchy. This is true whether you are trying to influence an individual or a group. Often your success as an influencer will rest on the consideration you gave to the informal organization.

1. What is the informal organization's structure?

2. Where are alliances and rivalries within the structure and between the informal and formal structure?

   ■ What do these alliances and rivalries tell you about how best to approach the person or group you need/want to influence?

3. Who are the stakeholders?

   ■ What will influence or motivate them to support or not support you?

Planning the Meeting

Generally it is not advisable to just show up at someone's door and begin the influencing process. Everyone has a significant number of high-priority projects they are trying to juggle on a daily basis. If you just show up and interrupt them with your agenda, you are likely to get a less than positive response.

1. When is the best time to influence this person or group?

2. Where is the best place to meet?

3. What materials will I need for the meeting (for example, handouts, or PowerPoint presentation)?

Once you have answered the relevant questions, it is time to organize the points you want to make and how best to make them. In many situations, at least when you are first learning how to effectively influence, it is helpful to create an outline and work from it. As long as you tell the person/group something to the effect of, "I want to make sure I don't forget anything important, so I'm going to work off an outline during some of our discussion," using the outline will generally not be seen negatively.

Step 2: Ascertain Readiness to Proceed

Now that you have taken some time to plan for the influencing meeting, it's time to meet with the person or people you want to influence. Professional courtesy and consideration is the key to this step. Approach the person or group you want to influence with the primary goal of providing an overview of what you want to talk to them about and determining when the best time would be to discuss the situation. You might want to say something such as, "I need a little bit of your time. I've noticed [problem, situation, or issue]. I've got some ideas on how to solve this, but I'd like to get your input and help. When would be a good time for us to talk about this?"

By doing this, you are already beginning your influencing process through demonstrating that you want to meet at your convenience as well as the other person's. This simple step puts the other person in a much more cooperative and positive frame of mind. It also allows him or her, if needed, some time to do some research prior to meeting with you. If the person wants to do some research, it does not mean that he or she is not willing to work with you; it only means that the person wants to come into the discussion prepared.

Step 3: Describe the Situation and Its Impact

When you actually sit down to talk to the person, you want to develop a mutual understanding of the problem and its impact. Until both you and the other person have the same understanding of the problem, situation, or issue, there is no way you can begin to work together to resolve it.

After you have gone through your research and planning process, it is often tempting to assume that you have also clearly defined what the problem, issue, or situation is. Never assume that you've come up with the root cause of the problem. When presenting the situation, it is best to start from the perspective, "My research has led me to believe that ____. However, I'd like to discuss it with you so that we know that we're working on the real problem rather than just a symptom of the problem, and that we agree on what the problem/issue/situation is." The goal here is for you and the other person to come to an agreement on what the problem, issue, or situation is.

Establish a mutual understanding of the problem's impact—past, present, and future—on you, the other person, specific teams, and/or the company as a whole. One of the biggest cautions here is not to place blame on anyone or anything. It simply does not matter who or what caused the situation to exist; the only thing that matters is what actions need to be taken to remedy the situation. As a result, this component of the process should simply be a review of the facts of the situation (past and present) and an estimation of the future implications should the problem/issue/situation not be resolved.

It's also important to use the correct wording when stating the problem. Table 8.2 gives examples of some alternative ways to word a problem statement.

Table 8.2: Use the Right Words

Instead of Saying...	Say...
"Obviously, we need to teach your shipping people to read and write. They can't seem to send a single product to the right customer."	"The company has seen a 6.11% increase in the shipping label errors over the past two months. It costs us an average of $39.95 to correct each error. Solving this problem will save the company more than $3,700 a month."

Instead of Saying...	Say...
"The sales department is, as usual, out of touch with production."	"There are three things happening that appear, at this time, to be interrelated: sales are up 11%, production is running at 100% capacity, and on-time delivery is down 9.25%. If these things are inter-related, the impact of this down the road will be _____."
"The people in quality aren't doing their job. They couldn't spot a product defect if it bit them!"	"In the last three months, there has been a 7.89% increase in calls to customer service reporting a defect in part X. If this continues, _____."

Step 4: Explain Your Recommended Action

During this step you should explain the following:

- What you want to do
- Why you believe it will solve the problem, issue, or situation
- What you need the other person/group to do
- What benefits will result for each of the impacted parties

The key in this step is helping the person or group you are trying to influence see the personal and organizational benefits that will result if they support and cooperate with you, and believe that those benefits will be realized. It is important to remember that most people, unless they feel that they are going to benefit in some way, are unlikely to agree to do what you want/need them to do.

Benefits are not a one-size-fits-all proposition. Different people look for different benefits. Table 8.3 provides some examples of benefits that might be realized. Regardless of the specific benefits you provide, the important thing to remember is that unless the cooperating parties will get a valued benefit, you are unlikely to be successful in your effort to influence them.

To open the discussion on resolving the situation, the approach you might want to take in presenting this step is to say, "What I'd like to do is _____. The benefits in this approach are _____. To do this, I need your help in _____. The benefits of us working together on this are _____."

Table 8.3: Example Benefits

Benefit	How to Achieve It
Reciprocity	Promise your assistance on a problem, issue, or situation that is important to them
Praise/recognition	Publicly let everyone know the valuable assistance the person/group provided.
	Send the person a thank-you e-mail or, better yet, a handwritten note thanking him or her for time, effort, energy, and contributions made.
	Nominate the person for employee of the month.
	Feature the person in an article in the company newsletter.
Work/job related	Ensure that the solution will make their job easier, faster, and so on.
	Provide the person with an opportunity to face a new challenge.
	Provide the person with an opportunity to learn something new.
Involvement	Let them have substantial say over what tasks they take on to resolve the situation rather than assigning them specific tasks.
Personal/Professional	Increased visibility in the team/department/ organization.
	Enhance his or her self-esteem.
	Provide the person the chance for inclusion.
	Enhance the person's reputation.
	Provide an opportunity to be of service to others.

Step 5: Ask for the Person's Input

Once you have proposed your preferred approach to addressing the situation, it's time to open the discussion to get the other person's or group's reaction, feedback, comments, ideas, and input. This is the time that your questioning skills and your listening skills will become even more important and will have a significant impact on your ability to influence the other person or group. You need to uncover the facts that the other person possesses relative to the problem, issue, or situation, as well as uncover the person's feelings about it and what you are asking him or her to do.

Although it is impossible to provide a list of specific questions that will help you uncover relevant information and feelings, you might want to ask questions that begin with phrases such as these:

- Who should be involved...?
- Who needs to know...?
- Who can tell/help us...?
- What do you know about...?
- What does _____ know about...?
- What would you do about...?
- What would you do when/if...?
- What evidence is there (facts are there) that...?
- What is the policy/procedure/SOP (standard operating procedure)/regulation...?
- What factors do we need to consider...?
- What do you think about...?
- When will you be able to...?
- When can you...?
- Where does it...?
- Where can we...?
- How do you feel about...?
- How would you handle...?

Step 6: Gain the Person's Support to Move Forward

Now that you have discussed the situation with the other person or group you are trying to influence, it's time to get their commitment to move forward. Often this is a simple question such as "Can I get your support and assistance to move forward on this?"

If the person/group has any remaining problems or concerns, they should surface at this point so that they can be addressed. This might mean a little give-and-take in order to move the solution forward. If there is still resistance, you might need to ask questions such as the following:

- "What would need to happen differently in order for you to help me move this solution forward?"

- "What concerns do you have about the approach we've discussed?"

- "What changes would need to be made in order for you to work with me to implement this solution?"

This is not a process of you completely caving in to the requests of the other person—or the other person caving in to your requests. It should be a give-and-take process where you say things such as, "OK, I'm willing to change X, but will you agree to do Y then?"

Step 7: Implement and Review the Success of the Approach Taken

Because you planned your approach; involved the person/group; listened to their ideas, concerns, and requests; and took a cooperative approach, this final two-phase step is simple. It is a matter of, first, putting the agreed-upon solution into place within the established timeframe. The second phase is following up to ensure that the solution you put into place actually solved the problem, issue, or situation. This means not only ensuring that the solution is working, but that all impacted parties are satisfied with the solution. If there are still problems, they need to be addressed, which might require cycling back to a previous step in the process and working through the steps from there on out.

As part of wrapping up the influencing process, it is important to thank the person/group you influenced. This is not only an issue of being polite, but also an issue of building goodwill and good working relationships throughout the organization.

Enhancing Your Success

Unfortunately, no process will give you all you need to be a successful influencer. To make your influencing skills even more effective, remember these six points:

1. **Choose your words carefully.** In particular, avoid using words such as "always" and "never" as well as emotionally laden

terms such as "pathetic" or "abysmal." Saying things like "Your consistently pathetic effort to ensure that proper procedures are followed is going to ruin this company. You never get things right" will not resolve the problem or contribute to a positive working environment. All these kinds of statements do is build a wall between you and the other person and delay the efforts to solve the problem.

Instead of saying, "You always miss the deadlines you agreed to," say "You agreed to get the customer service call report summary on Project J to me by the end of the day yesterday. What happened that you missed the deadline?" This approach is nonaccusatory and opens the possibility that there is a legitimate reason for the person missing the deadline.

2. **Validate the other person's/group's feelings.** If you approach influencing with the perspective that your facts and feelings are the only acceptable and "right" ones, you might end up facing resistance that will be difficult—if not impossible—to work through. Everyone has a right to their feelings and their take on the facts. If you are going to influence someone to see things from your point of view and support the approach you want to take, you will need to understand where the other person/group is coming from and discuss all viewpoints openly and honestly.

3. **Handle resistance appropriately.** Sometimes when you're faced with resistance, the temptation is to push forward with your agenda harder, more aggressively, and with less tact and decorum. Often this only results in the other person pushing back harder. When this happens, the result is often that the issue doesn't get resolved or doesn't get resolved to either party's satisfaction. When you are faced with resistance, you might want to

- Call a break so that you and the other party can get away from the situation and clear your heads.

- Work with the other party to identify areas you have in common, rather than arguing over what you view differently. Often this simple step will help both you and the other person/group realize that you are closer to agreement than you realize and that your differences are minor.

- Take the emotion out of the situation. There are times when our emotions tend to get the better of us and we start saying things and making decisions based on our emotional reaction to what we have heard. In these situations, it might be helpful for you and the other person/group to agree to focus only on the known, provable facts relative to the situation for a period of time.

- Put emotion into the situation. If you have been focusing too strongly on the facts of the situation, open a discussion about the emotional aspects of what you and the other party are stuck on.

4. **Look for creative ways to get unstuck.** In some situations, you will have to negotiate a different solution than what you originally proposed. When this happens, you might reach a point where you and the other party are unable to reach an agreement on something required to move forward. If this happens, look for ways around the problem using techniques such as the following:

    - Use an analogy, simile, or metaphor around what you are stuck on. For example, you might ask "How would [famous person, cartoon character, fictional character, and so on] solve this problem?" or "How is this problem like a ___ [hot dog, lifeboat, merry-go-round, or other noun]?" The creativity involved in answering the question may be just what is needed to get you unstuck.

    - Bring out some toys and just play for a while. Keep a box filled with different toys such as stress balls, soft building blocks, flexible/bendable plastic links and blocks—and even rubber chickens—any of which can enhance creativity.

Vasquez Uses Play to Beat Stress

Vasquez keeps a box filled with toys in his office. When he started with the company, he told his co-workers that he found that playing with them was helpful not only when he was stressed out, but when he was stuck on something. He told his co-workers to feel free to borrow any of the toys when they wanted, just to make sure they returned them so others could use them. Today, it's not unusual for a co-worker to walk into his office, rummage around in the box, pull out a toy, and leave. If he's there, he and his co-worker exchange knowing looks—and often a little laugh.

- Talk a short walk outside, sit near the pond/water fountain for a few minutes, go to a different part of the building where you can look outside at some enjoyable scenery for a few minutes, and so on. Sometimes just physically walking away from the detail you're stuck on for a few minutes will result in you coming back with a different perspective.

- Bring in someone who has no vested interest in the problem or the solution and get their ideas. Sometimes people who have little knowledge of and interest in the situation or solution are able to give a unique perspective. Although their perspective might not be the answer to what you are stuck on, it might be just what was needed to get you to look at the challenge differently.

5. **Learn to see both sides.** When you feel that you and the other person are on opposite sides of the fence, try walking a mile in their shoes. That is, try to come up with some facts, ideas, and perspectives that support the other person's comments or views. When you are able to understand where the other person is coming from, you're more likely to find an approach that is acceptable to both of you.

6. **Follow through.** This should go without saying because you are the person who is the influencer, but make sure that you live up to your agreements. This not only ensures that the problem is resolved, but helps build a stronger working relationship with the other party.

Conclusion: The Power of Influencing

In today's organizations, regardless of the level you are at, very little gets accomplished without some amount of influencing. The person who learns to do it well

- Builds credibility and respect within the organization
- Is viewed as a fair and open-minded individual
- Establishes long-term, mutually beneficial relationships with others

In short, effective influencers are people who are likely to be successful throughout their career because of their ability to work well with a wide range of individuals and gain their cooperation in a positive and constructive manner.

CHAPTER 9   **Maximizing Your Results**

Everyone wants to be viewed as a valuable contributor, someone who makes a positive difference at work. You can maximize your results by building and using skills such as focusing on internal customer needs, meeting commitments, following up, and setting goals. By using these skills, you can increase your impact at work and have more of your ideas accepted and implemented. Beyond that, you will look forward to going to work, and actually have fun while you are there. Enjoying work and feeling proud of what you do are important in light of the amount of time you spend at work. The energy and time you invest in this chapter can also provide a lasting payout of increased satisfaction and pride in your job.

Become an Expert in Job-Related Skills

As you are developing skills for getting ahead, you cannot overlook job-related skills that are specific to the job that you do. Your boss and co-workers are counting on you to do your part. Your approach to learning the job initially will establish lasting impressions in others' minds, so you want these impressions to be positive.

The problem is that your new environment can be intimidating. Remember your first weeks as a freshman in high school. Imagine that when you walked into each class during the day, you were the only freshman, surrounded by upperclassmen. This awkward situation is how your new job can feel. Everyone else knows each other and knows what is expected.

In order to be viewed as qualified and competent, make sure to

- Be open to learning.

- Avoid being aloof or overly confident.

- Ask co-workers how to do something if you are confused.

- Ask your boss to identify one or two key contact persons to go to when questions arise.

- When you ask questions, listen and take notes so that you don't have to keep coming back with the same question.

- Assemble a notebook or file with key information and resources. Continue to update it throughout your time on the job. Some people refer to this type of resource as a job control book.

- Be proactive in asking for feedback on what you are doing well and in what areas you can improve. Ask for specific examples if you are told something vague, such as "you need to be more of a team player."

Learn What Is Important Through Customer Focus

To gain a sharper focus and new sense of importance for what you do, you must frame your work around your customers' needs and expectations of you. You have two sets of customers: those who work outside of your organization and those who work inside the organization. It is more natural to think about focusing on meeting the needs of your external customers, those outside of your organization. Yet, you also have internal customers: your colleagues, your boss, and even people who report to you.

Thinking about your colleagues and direct reports as internal customers can require some humility. This chapter addresses the internal customers specifically because they are often overlooked. However, the principles in this chapter also apply to your external customers.

How Do You Impact Your Internal Customers?

Completing the columns in the exercise on page 183 will clarify the ways that you impact your internal customers. In column one, list your work products and services. These are the tasks and projects that you are assigned. Then, in column two, identify for each set of products and services the people within your organization who receive and depend on them. To complete this exercise, use column three to capture what is important to the recipients relative to the product or service they receive. An example is provided to get you started.

Exercise: Internal Customer Identification

My Tasks and Projects	The Recipient(s)	What Is Important to the Recipients
Organize monthly staff meeting	My boss The people attending the meeting	Being able to provide input to the agenda. Receiving assignments at least one week before the meeting. Knowing the decisions made and next steps identified during the meeting.

In order to complete column three you might have needed to make some guesses or assumptions because you haven't specifically asked your internal customers what is important to them. If you needed to guess, a logical next step is to informally ask your customers what is important about the work product or service that you provide them. Although you might be tempted to confirm what is important via e-mail, it is more valuable to engage in an in-person, two-way discussion. Doing so can help you reach a deeper understanding of their true expectations. Either they will confirm your guesses, or they will give you new insights into their needs. If you haven't had this type of conversation before, you will find that your co-workers will probably react very positively. In addition, you might uncover other gems, like the examples of surprises in the following list. All of these findings were the result of informal needs discussions with internal customers.

- Brenda worked as an administrative assistant for a large municipality. One of Brenda's responsibilities was to generate a report each month and send it to a distribution list of 10 people. She had never received feedback about the report from her internal customers. During the discussions that Brenda initiated, she learned that over time the report had lost its relevance. Although each of the 10 people immediately discarded the report upon receipt, no one had thought to tell Brenda. Also, Brenda was able to learn about these individuals' unmet needs and folded meeting these needs into her regular duties as she stopped generating the unneeded report. Brenda found that the new responsibilities caused her work to be more interesting and rewarding.

- Rob and Jennifer were customer service managers who had worked together in side-by-side offices for about a year. During a discussion over coffee, Rob learned that Jennifer preferred face-to-face conversations to resolve issues rather than using e-mail correspondence. Rob agreed that it had been ludicrous to send countless e-mails back and forth rather than just walking a few yards to talk in person. By simply changing their communication method, Rob and Jennifer were able to resolve differences more quickly and previous unproductive conflicts were eliminated.

- Keisha was one of six people receiving a quarterly data analysis from Mike. Upon receipt, she reformatted it and added information to help her decision-making. Mike had access to this information, and could easily have saved Keisha time by adding it. During a discussion that Mike initiated with Keisha, he learned about the reformatting. Mike then spoke with the other five people receiving the analysis and learned that the modification would help them also. So, he instituted the change.

- Carol always held the weekly operations review with her management team every Friday at 10:00 a.m. At the end of one of the meetings, Carol overheard a couple of her staff members complaining that they couldn't resolve customer issues on Fridays because they were in the review during the time it was easiest to reach customers. This surprised Carol because when she first began holding the weekly meetings, the team had said that they preferred starting at 10:00 a.m. So, with this new information, at the next meeting Carol asked her team what time they would prefer to begin the review meetings. All 10 individuals asked to start the meeting at 8:00 a.m. for the same reason she had overheard the previous week. This earlier start time was also better for Carol, for similar reasons.

The common thread in all these examples is that individuals had been staying with the status quo because it *seemed* to be working. After they met with their internal customers, they uncovered some new and interesting information. Change isn't *always* appropriate, yet it makes sense when modifications result in better meeting the needs of your customers. Asking a few simple questions of your customers and then engaging in a two-way conversation with them can lead to improvements that are well worth the minimal time investment.

You Depend on Your Customers, Too

In many situations with internal customers, there is a reciprocal relationship; in other words, you are both customer and supplier to others at work. For example, Arturo provides his colleague Frank monthly sales and cost figures that Frank needs at a certain time and in a readable, usable format. When Arturo addresses Frank's needs of timeliness and readability, Frank is better equipped to provide others, including Arturo, an analysis that assists with their decision-making. On the other hand, if Arturo lowers the priority of Frank's request and misses the deadline or does a partial, sloppy job, then most likely what Arturo receives back from Frank will not be as useful to him. Frank is not doing this out of spite. Instead, in order for Frank to meet his customers' needs, his needs must first be met. These interdependencies with internal customers are important to acknowledge and discuss. Remember this phrase: *follow through* when others depend on you, and *follow up* when your success depends on others.

Conflict with Your Customers

There are times when conflict occurs with internal customers due to unmet expectations or expectations that seem to be unrealistic. For example, if a co-worker comes across as demanding and unyielding when asking for information by a certain time, you might become upset and want to lash back. Or, it might anger you if you asked two colleagues for information a week ago that you needed to meet a deadline, and when you follow up with them about it they say they forgot. It is important to handle these situations professionally. Avoiding conflict is not an option because it can lead to missing important external customer expectations. In addition, letting problem situations go unresolved can harm your reputation. Chapter 7 provides more information on handling tough conflict situations.

Set Up a System for Meeting Commitments and Following Up with Others

Now that you have clarified what is important to your internal customers, you most likely have raised their expectations of you. This outcome is positive because you want to be viewed as a responsible, credible person who can be counted on to meet commitments. The challenge now is to establish a means for consistently meeting all of your customers' needs.

Methods for Tracking Tasks

There are many approaches for tracking work tasks and expectations, ranging from a technical device such as a personal digital assistant, to a simple handwritten approach such as a daily checklist. The key is to use something that fits your style and works for you. Notice the systems that your friends and colleagues use. Try out different techniques. If one doesn't work, try another until you are satisfied with your results. Perhaps a hybrid system would work best for you, combining electronic and paper devices or using elements of various paper approaches.

Bernard Tries a Different Tracking Method

Bernard had been using a daily assignment book through high school and his first year of college to track his assignments, tests, and activities. This method had worked well for him. Then, one of his professors mentioned in class how he kept on top of his work. He simply used a piece of paper that he put in his back pocket each day, writing down work to do as he went through the day, adding and deleting from the list, and tossing the paper at the end of the day.

Bernard respected his professor and thought this sounded like an easier approach. So, Bernard tried it out for a few weeks and learned that what worked for the professor, didn't work for him. He went back to the approach that had worked for him for the previous five years because he preferred having an ongoing record rather than just a daily one. Trying a different technique gave Bernard a new appreciation for the importance of tracking and following up on assignments. Bernard also learned the value of testing changes, an important aspect of continual improvement.

Think about the system you are using now to keep track of work tasks, and answer the questions in the following exercise. If you aren't using any one system now, then answer the questions for what you did in previous school or work situations. Answering these questions will provide insights to help improve your ability to meet commitments.

Exercise: Analyzing Your Method for Meeting Commitments

1. What do you do now to help you keep track of and meet commitments?

   _____

   _____

2. How long have you used this approach?

   _____

3. What do you like about this approach?

   _____

   _____

4. What do you dislike about this approach?

   _____

   _____

5. What is your track record of meeting the following commitments?

   ■ Deadlines_____

(continued)

(continued)

- Meeting preparation_____
- Scheduling of work_____
- Returning phone messages_____
- Responding to e-mail messages_____
6. How might you improve on your current track record?

_____

_____

Hopefully, answering the questions in the preceding exercise enabled you to come up with some helpful new insights. Many times the solutions to your challenges rest inside of you. You just need time to think to let them surface.

Determine Your Priorities

Once you have established an effective method for tracking tasks, it is important to have a means for prioritizing your work. Prioritizing is simply determining the order in which you address work tasks. There can be a temptation to start with the tasks you enjoy the most, or those you are most comfortable doing. Yet, these tasks might not be the most appropriate. At the start of a new job, it can be helpful to get your boss's input on general priorities. After a while, you will want to be able to do this independently because your boss might not always be available, and might not want to have to do this for you.

When assigning an order to your daily tasks, ask yourself how important and urgent they are. A task's importance is determined by its impact on your organization and your customers. So, filing is not as important as making sales calls. Urgency is determined based on the immediacy of attention that is required. For example, if you have a meeting at 2:00 p.m. today to present monthly cost figures and you haven't calculated the figures yet, the preparation for the presentation is an urgent task. If the presentation were scheduled for next week rather than today, this task would still be important, but not yet urgent.

Assign the highest priority to tasks that are both important and urgent. Next complete those that are important but not urgent. For tasks that are urgent, yet not important, ask yourself what would happen if you didn't complete the task. The answer will clarify what to do. For example, if you have been asked to attend a meeting this morning that is not important to your job, you might end up calling to say you won't attend because you have something urgent that you need to do.

As you are prioritizing, also remember the impact you have on your co-workers. Sometimes your attention to a project is required so that your co-workers can deliver on customer expectations. Unfortunately, it can be easy to put off these types of projects, which can strain interpersonal relationships and create stress. In the early days of your job, if you have questions about prioritizing, see your boss or an experienced co-worker.

Maybe Your Mindset Is the Problem

Sometimes the cause of missing commitments is one's mindset rather than the system that they are using. Have you ever seen individuals using the latest technology, busily inputting the next scheduled meeting and follow-up tasks into a handheld device, who regularly miss meetings and fail to follow through on what they promised? If meeting commitments is a challenge for you, first determine whether you want to change. Is the gain that results from changing worth the possible pain caused by the additional effort?

Possible benefits to changing your mindset include the following:

- Being viewed as someone who can be counted on for results and follow-through.
- Being given preferred projects and assignments.
- Being given additional responsibility and thus an opportunity for greater impact in the organization.

Know Your Limitations and Abilities

In addition to having a system for keeping track of commitments, it is also important to be able to assess your own capability, and to not take on more than what you can realistically do. Many people find it hard to say no and to push back on their customers' requests. Yet, by not negotiating deadlines, they end up missing commitments and having to explain the situation to their customers, which is a much more painful discussion. Why not increase your credibility by confidently agreeing to what you *know* you can deliver? Only make promises that you know you can keep. If you have any doubt, don't promise it.

It takes time and experience to develop a successful approach to making and meeting commitments. Your responses to the following two questions are important indicators of how well you manage your commitments.

- When your boss asks you to complete a new project in two days, how do you react?

- When your co-workers ask you when you can get back to them with the information they are requesting, how do you determine your answers?

One key to help with this process is the ability to reliably predict the time it takes to accomplish various tasks. Being aware and noticing how long your typical work tasks require will help you more confidently predict these times.

Do you want to be viewed as someone who can be depended upon to deliver what you promise? You have probably heard the phrase "under-promise and over-deliver." Following these words of advice will improve your credibility.

Become a Confident Decision-Maker

To meet commitments, you also need to be decisive and a confident decision-maker. There are approaches that can help you make better decisions while developing these skills. You have made countless decisions in your life so far, including the important decision of accepting your current job. Think back on this decision and answer the following questions:

1. How difficult or easy was it to decide to accept your job?

2. What factors helped you to decide to accept the job (for example, the creativity involved in the work, the personality of your boss, the relaxed work environment, or the location)?

3. What factors caused you to hesitate to accept the job (for example, the long work hours, the starting salary, or the uncertainty of the industry)?

4. Who did you turn to for advice?

When making decisions, we all use criteria or values. Your answers to questions 2 and 3 provide an idea of what criteria and values were involved in your job decision. You might not always be aware of these factors at the time, yet deciding on these factors ahead of time can make your decisions better ones.

As you encounter decisions that seem difficult, begin with a quick analysis of the pros and cons of a course of action.

Jerry Decides Whether to Have an After-Work Activity

Jerry needed to decide whether to have an after-work activity for his department. His analysis follows.

Reasons to Do It:	Reasons Not to Do It:
Build camaraderie	Difficult to schedule
Done in the past	Cost factor
People want to do it	Time to plan it

After identifying and thinking about the pros and cons, Jerry was clear that he wanted to proceed with the after-work activity for the department.

Decision-making clarity doesn't always occur. If, after completing your lists of pros and cons, you still are confused about what to do, talk it through with a co-worker. Sometimes verbalizing a possible decision helps to clarify what is most important to you. Or, answer these questions:

1. What is the worst that would happen if I do nothing?
2. What is the worst that would happen if I proceed?

These answers can also help you decide.

There may be times when you need to decide amongst several different alternatives. You can use a matrix to list the solutions in the far left column and the criteria in each of the remaining columns. Rate each solution using your criteria, and see which solution is optimal. Establish criteria that make sense for the type of decision you are making.

Jerry Chooses from Among Several Options

Once Jerry decided to proceed with the department after-work activity, he needed to decide from among several options what type of activity it would be. These options came from a brainstorming meeting of the department. Jerry could have rated each of the options by criteria. Instead, he simply assessed whether the solution met the criteria (+) or did not meet the criteria (−).

(continued)

(continued)

	Cost	Time	Impact	Ease
Great America Theme Park	–	+	–	+
Local forest preserve	+	–	+	–
Dave and Buster's	+	+	+	+

After going through this analysis, Jerry decided to ask his department members what they thought about going to Dave and Buster's. They overwhelmingly thought it was a great idea, and agreed to "chip in" a small amount each to help cover the cost.

Commitment-Management Scenarios

Below are some suggested responses to two different scenarios. As you review them, think about how you can apply the suggestions to your situation.

Scenario One: Interaction with the Boss

Boss: "I need this new market realignment project done in two days. We need to move on it quickly. Here is the CD with all the files, contact names and numbers, and background information you will need. I expect you to get started on this right away."

You: "This sounds like a great opportunity. Thanks. I want to make sure I am clear about the project requirements and how this affects the priority of my other projects."

Boss: "No problem—I can understand that the other projects you are working on might be delayed slightly."

You: "It would help me if you could explain to John and Linda that each of their projects will be delayed until this new project is complete. It could be a delay of two to three days, depending on how long the new project requires. I am sure they will understand and appreciate hearing it from you."

Boss: "I have no problem telling them, but what do you mean depending on how long the project requires? I told you I need it done in two days."

You: "I understand that it is a high-priority project. For that reason, I am sure you agree that it is important I put together a well-thought-out, high-quality recommendation. So, I would like to have some time to look at the project's scope and let you know whether I need additional resources to meet the deadline."

Boss: "You know that I can't give you any additional resources."

You: "Well, I thought I would just check, in light of the project's priority. Because there are no resources, what is magical about two days? Is any flexibility possible?"

Boss: "Well, I need to put together a recommendation for the VP of Operations by her next visit, which is in three weeks."

You: "Well that is helpful to know. Let me get right on this and put together a detailed plan that allows time for you to give me feedback on my draft and for me to finalize it and prepare a presentation for the VP's visit. I'll get that schedule to you within the next day."

What happened with this conversation? You learned from your boss what the real deadline was by asking some relevant questions. You discovered that the VP is expecting a presentation on the recommendations. And, your boss will help in renegotiating deadlines with your other customers, instead of you trying to meet all the deadlines, perhaps unsuccessfully.

Scenario Two: Interaction with a Co-worker

Co-worker: "I need last month's line efficiencies. When can you get back to me with them?"

You: "Well, it would help to know how you will be using the numbers, and when you need them."

Co-worker: "Well, I am writing the monthly report for the plant manager. It's not due for another week, but I thought I'd see if I could get it done now."

You: "Thanks for giving me some lead time. I can get it to you by the end of the day tomorrow. Will that work? Also, would it be helpful to have a comparison to each of the previous six months' results? I can easily get that information for you also."

Co-worker: "Sure, the end of tomorrow will be fine. And, those comparisons are a great idea. Thanks."

Again, asking clarifying questions helps you to do a better job of understanding the true need and assessing when and how you can meet the need. The next key is to make sure that you write down the task and its due date, so that you can deliver on what you promised.

Strategies to Overcome Procrastination

Procrastination is putting off or delaying tasks. Everyone is human, and so has bouts of procrastination. You put off completing a task to another day, week, or month. In the back of your mind, you are hoping that the task will disappear or get done by someone else. Unfortunately, your procrastination can lead to disappointing your customers, missing deadlines, and hurting your reputation.

Juan Procrastinates Because He Is Uncertain How to Perform the Task

After five years with the company, Juan was promoted to a new position in another department. He was excited, but a bit nervous, because of all the unknowns he would be encountering in his new job and work environment. In his previous position he worked on clearly defined, short-term tasks. His promotion required him to excel with projects that were longer term and less well defined. In addition, he didn't know anyone in the new department, which had a predominantly female workforce. He was accustomed to working in a mostly male work environment. Juan was coping with multiple changes.

During his first week, Juan's boss, Carrie, sent him an e-mail, asking him to organize a training program for new managers. Juan was stunned by the vagueness of Carrie's request, and had no idea where to begin. He wasn't comfortable asking his new boss, who resided in another state, for guidance. So, Juan put the project on the back burner, waiting until he had a chance to ask his boss about it without appearing to be incompetent.

Carrie came into town a month later. During her meeting with Juan she asked for an update on the training program. After a bit of stumbling, Juan came clean and expressed his confusion about what Carrie wanted. Carrie asked Juan what he was confused about, and Juan asked some clarifying questions. Through this process Juan learned that what Carrie really wanted was for Juan to develop an orientation process for the managers to follow when they joined the organization. Carrie gave Juan the names of two people to contact to get ideas about how it was done now and how it could be improved. Juan was much more comfortable about moving forward, and in fact got started on it the next morning.

Think about the times you have procrastinated in the past as you answer the questions in the following exercise.

Exercise: Reflections on Procrastination

1. On what tasks and projects have you procrastinated?

   _____

   _____

   _____

2. Why have you put off completing these tasks and projects?

   _____

   _____

   _____

3. What finally prompted you to begin work on these tasks and projects?

   _____

   _____

   _____

4. Think of a specific time you procrastinated. What was the negative impact to you, to others, or to your department?

   _____

   _____

   _____

Sometimes procrastination can lead to positive results. Perhaps by holding off on starting a project, you minimized wasted time because the project ended up being cancelled. Or, by waiting until you received critical data you minimized rework in calculations. Although sometimes these benefits do occur, waiting for them to happen in all cases is not worth the risk to your reputation. If you become known as someone who cannot be counted on, you will not feel comfortable working in that environment for long, and surely will not be proud of what you do. Table 9.1 provides some possible strategies that you can try when you find yourself procrastinating.

Table 9.1: Strategies to Overcome Procrastination

Nature of the Task	Possible Approaches
Large, complex, and beyond your capabilities	Break down a large project into smaller, more manageable chunks or action steps. Organize the steps into a logical order of completion. Identify other resources to assist you.
Routine or boring work that you don't like doing	Identify others who might enjoy the work. Consider delegating to them. If there is no one else, schedule to complete the task at the beginning of the day. Schedule to complete similar tasks all at once.
Ill-defined work that may require more time than it is worth	Ask your customers clarifying questions about what they are expecting. Bounce ideas off colleagues.
Requires risk-taking or stepping out of your comfort zone	Set a goal or deadline and promise yourself a reward. Share the challenge with a colleague you trust and have that person play the role of supporter.
Requires working with people who are difficult	Determine the impact or cost of procrastinating. Identify what you could learn from the situation.
Requires working alone	Find time to talk about the project with others, to get their ideas and perspectives.

Samantha Overcomes Procrastinating About Making Cold Calls

Samantha brought many strengths to her sales position, yet procrastination had haunted her since she was in high school. Samantha and her boss had collaboratively established a goal of 10 cold phone calls per day and five follow-up calls daily. In the follow-up calls, Samantha was to reconnect with the potential buyers whom she had cold-called two weeks earlier. Samantha's strength was face-to-face selling, and she disliked making these calls. Yet, they were needed for her to obtain in-person meetings and thus build her sales volume. Samantha tended to put off making these calls, resulting in slower sales growth and uncomfortable meetings with her boss.

Samantha realized that in order to be successful and meet her career goals, she needed to try various strategies to help her stop procrastinating about making the sales calls. Instead of sprinkling the calls throughout the day, Samantha scheduled her day so that she made the follow-up calls at a certain time each morning, and the 10 initial cold calls toward the end of each day. Scheduling the calls in this way helped them become part of her routine. She also made a pact with another sales representative that each would work on meeting their calling goals more consistently, and give each other reminders and encouragement when they met for lunch. Talking each day at lunch about their morning calls established some additional accountability. After they both met their goals for a two-week period, they celebrated with a special lunch. The learning from this experience helped Samantha when she was promoted and needed to coach her direct reports in making their phone calls.

Make a Difference with Effective Goal Setting

Unfortunately, many people new to the world of work find themselves unable to set big-picture goals. Whether it's because they have a new boss or one that is too busy, new hires are often not aware that they need to go beyond fulfilling their basic job functions to set goals for making a positive difference. You should be ready to do this after you have completed initial training on your job. While you are going through your training, you might be able to identify some areas you would like to focus on for improvement.

Jason's Lack of Goal-Setting Hurts His Performance

Jason's first employer out of college, a college admissions department, had high expectations for him. He graduated with highest honors and had held leadership positions in organizations throughout college. Like other new college graduates, Jason had a challenging transition to work life, beginning with having to get up by 6:00 a.m. each day to get to work on time. In addition, Jason's boss, Paula, who had just been promoted into her position, was struggling with her own transition. After Jason completed his training, he focused on his job responsibilities—completing the tasks that were part of his job description consistently and accurately. So, he was disappointed a few months later when Paula told him that his performance was not up to the organization's expectations. Jason had been focusing on his day-to-day

(continued)

(continued)

responsibilities, accepting the status quo. He had not considered setting goals that reflected ways he could make a difference in his department's results. Jason wasn't sure how to respond to this feedback, and
his boss didn't seem to have time to provide him much help.

Goals are a means for making a difference in your job. They provide
structure and discipline for achieving your vision. To begin, think
about the ideal state of your job—how you would like things to be.
Sometimes identifying problem areas that you are able to influence
can help clarify the ideal state you would like to achieve.

Setting Goals

Once you have thought through some of the problem areas and what
you want to achieve, you can brainstorm your goals. Remember that
your goals need to serve you and your needs, and be realistic and
practical. Too often people set lofty goals that are just filed away
instead of becoming a guide to achieving results in the job.

Jason Sets a Goal

One of Jason's many responsibilities was the coordination of campus
tours for potential new students and their parents. He seemed to
spend much of his time rescheduling and filling in for the volunteer
tour guides who were calling him, sometimes at the last minute, to say
they couldn't handle a tour. In addition, he wasn't sure about the quality of the tour guides' presentations. He remembered that when he
was deciding on colleges and visiting campuses, the tour guides had
quite an impact on his view of the college. Jason's vision was for the
tour guides to cause potential students to want to come to the university. Also, he wanted to stop spending time rescheduling tour
guides so that he could instead focus on the quality of the tours and
his other responsibilities. So, Jason set a goal to improve the quality of
campus tours given to potential students.

For goals to help you make a positive difference, they need to be
motivating to you. Goals tend to be motivational when

- You can get excited and energized about working to achieve
  them.

- They are crucial to your job success.

- They are connected to your vision of what you want to
  achieve.

Establishing Key Measures of Success

You can't stop with just a goal statement if you want to make a difference. The next step is to establish key measures of success and a means for tracking them.

Jason Selects Measures for Success

Jason decided to use the following as his measures:

- The results of the feedback forms completed after each tour, to be tracked monthly

- The percentage of students who took campus tours and decided to attend the university, to be tracked monthly

- The number of cancellations by tour guides, to be tracked weekly

After establishing targets for each measure, Jason could begin tracking his results as he implemented his plan.

Creating an Action Plan

The next step is to create an action plan by breaking your goal statement into manageable action steps. The way to identify action steps is to answer the question "How am I going to accomplish this goal?"

Jason Creates an Action Plan

At this point, Jason was ready to create an action plan. Jason's brainstormed action steps for improving the quality of campus tours included the following:

1. Put together a set of hiring criteria for tour guides.

2. Re-interview current tour guides and advertise for potential new guides, using the new criteria.

3. Create a short training program for all of the tour guides.

4. Share the expectation that if someone can't handle a scheduled tour, they are responsible for getting a replacement. Explain this expectation during the interviews and reinforce it during the training.

5. Put in place a short feedback form for all visitors to complete after each tour.

Setting Dates for Your Action Steps

You then need to establish realistic start dates and completion dates for all the action steps. When establishing dates, it is common to identify additional activities to be completed. It is better to have a longer list of detailed, specific activities than a shorter list of broad, general actions. Adding more details will help you complete the steps and thus achieve your goal.

Jason Identifies Additional Action Steps

The third action step from Jason's initial list was to create a short training program for all the tour guides. When putting together completion dates, Jason broke this one action step down further into these five additional steps:

1. Contact other universities and find out about their training programs.

2. Assemble a handout.

3. Get approval on the handout from Paula.

4. Schedule the training session and reserve the room and equipment.

5. Prepare notes for the training session.

The action steps need to be in a logical order. Before finalizing your dates, ensure that your steps are also sequenced logically.

It is natural when establishing completion dates to be more aggressive than realistic. Consider your first stab at dates as a draft. Then go back over them, keeping in mind your job responsibilities and any special circumstances at work.

Remember: It is much better to beat a realistic completion date than to miss an aggressive one. Also, providing a cushion will ensure that you can deliver excellent results with each of your action steps, rather than hurrying through them.

Gathering Feedback

It's essential to gather feedback from your boss and colleagues on your action steps and success measures. Gathering feedback creates more buy-in and provides additional creativity and new insights.

Jason Gets Feedback and Overcomes Some Roadblocks

Jason updated his plan after receiving feedback from Paula and the current tour guides. He then began implementing the action steps.

Jason ran into some unforeseen obstacles that delayed his plan slightly. One of the obstacles was a result of Jason being new to the organization. He was not aware that he needed approval from the human resource department on his hiring criteria. When he encountered this roadblock, Jason angrily complained to Paula about the delay. She explained to him the value of the human resource perspective, and coached him to learn from this barrier rather than being deenergized by it.

Based on some college intern experiences, Jason had developed the skill of anticipating possible barriers. He thought he might not hear from all the universities he chose to contact if he sent a blind e-mail. So, he had Paula help him get the names of his counterparts so that he could call them. This additional step helped him with his goal, and also broadened his professional network. As he completed his phone calls, Jason was reminded of the need to be open to new ways of doing things.

Goal-Setting Summary

Table 9.2 provides a recap of the goal-setting process.

Table 9.2: The Goal-Setting Process

Step	Tips and Techniques
Think of the ideal state or vision of your job responsibilities, and the problems you want to eliminate. Create an initial goal statement that describes what you want to to accomplish.	Write down your goals and look at them regularly. Always have your goals in mind.
Decide on key measures of success and track and report on them regularly.	Do periodic status checks. As appropriate, post charts or graphs of your results. Proudly share your successes.

(continued)

(continued)

Table 9.2: The Goal-Setting Process

Step	Tips and Techniques
Create an action plan of steps that will help you achieve your goal.	Update the plan as needed. Anticipate potential barriers that might arise.
Establish start dates and realistic completion dates for all the action steps.	Keep track of your progress in completing steps and celebrate your progress.

As you approach goal setting, remember the following suggestions:

- Gain support from your boss and others affected by your work.

- Organize activities that are needed to achieve your goal.

- Aspire to your vision when identifying the goals you want to achieve.

- Learn from others and from your own experiences as you are creating and completing your action plan.

- Spell out ways to overcome probable barriers as you think through your action steps.

Conclusion: Key Points to Remember About Maximizing Your Results

- Establish a job-control notebook or file that stores information and resources about your job.

- Take time to understand your internal customers' needs and the reasons behind those needs. Ensure that you have a two-way conversation.

- Acknowledge the interdependency with your internal customers. Follow through when others depend on you and follow up when your success depends on others.

- Find a system that works for you to ensure that you meet the commitments that you make to others. Test various options and select one that fits you best, or create a hybrid system.

- Assign the highest priority to completing tasks that are important and urgent.

- When you receive a new project or activity with a quick deadline and you are concerned about the impact on other projects, ask questions of the person giving you the project to clarify the true need.

- To be more decisive, identify the pros and cons of a course of action.

- After you have completed your initial job training, set goals for how you want to make a positive difference in your work.

- Be realistic in establishing completion dates for your action steps.

- Be open to changing your goals when it makes sense. Ensure that the goals are serving you by helping you make a positive difference at work.

- Remember that many times the solutions to your challenges rest inside of you. Take time to contemplate and let them surface.

INDEX

ABOUT THE AUTHORS

Diane C. Decker has extensive experience coaching groups and individuals to improve their effectiveness. Before starting Quality Transitions in 1994, she worked in customer service, human resource development, and operations management with Procter & Gamble. Ms. Decker has a B.S. in Industrial Management from Purdue University and an MBA from Xavier University. She is a certified Creatrix™ Consultant, providing innovation assessment and improvement. She has served as a judge for the Illinois Manufacturers' Association Team Excellence Awards and as an examiner for the Lincoln Award for Business Excellence. Ms. Decker has served on the board of the Association of Consultants to Nonprofits. She is a certified Women's Business Enterprise with the City of Chicago. Her work on the value of laughter and fun in the workplace has been profiled in newspapers across the country, including the *Chicago Tribune*, the *Christian Science Monitor*, and the *Wall Street Journal*.

Victoria A. Hoevemeyer has more than 20 years of organizational development and management/leadership development experience as both an internal and external consultant. She has a bachelor's degree in social work from Western Michigan University and a master's degree in organizational behavior and development from Eastern Michigan University. She has provided organizational development and training for service, transportation, retail, health care, education, building materials, government, and light and heavy manufacturing organizations in California, Arizona, Colorado, Michigan, and Illinois. She is the author of *High Impact Interview Questions: 701 Behavioral-Based Questions to Find the Right Person for Every Job* (American Management Association, 2005).

Marianne Rowe-Dimas has more than 20 years of management experience in marketing, sales, and customer service. She has a strong background in employee hiring, training, and assessment. As a corporate vice president, she was responsible for corporate identity building, business communications, and customer retention. Ms. Rowe-Dimas currently owns and manages The Image Factor. As an image consultant and business trainer, she helps her clients look more professional—both on paper and in person. She provides training in the areas of business writing, presentation skills, professional image enhancement, communication skills, business-casual dress, business and social etiquette, and self-marketing. Her clients include companies in the airline, entertainment, finance, food service, health care, manufacturing, pharmaceutical, sports, technology, and travel industries. She has also served associations and not-for-profit agencies. Ms. Rowe-Dimas holds a B.A. from the University of Illinois, Urbana. She received her certification as an image consultant from the internationally known London Image Institute. She is also certified on AchieveGlobal's Leadership Suite. Ms. Rowe-Dimas has been published in *Training Today* magazine. Her expertise has been sought out, with her quotes appearing in major newspapers and *Newsweek* magazine. She is an in-demand speaker and appears regularly on cable television's Library Channel.